making memory
creating britain's first holocaust centre

making memory

creating britain's first holocaust centre

stephen d. smith

making memory
creating britain's first holocaust centre
by Stephen D. Smith

Published in Great Britain by
Quill Press
Woodlands, Main Street, Kirton,
Newark, Nottinghamshire. NG22 9LP

First published 1999
Revised edition 2002

British Library Catalogue in Publication Data
A catalogue record for this book is available from the British
Library

ISBN 0-9536280-9-4

Cover Photograph: Stephen and James Smith by Glen Powell

Design and Production: The Holocaust Centre Design Studio

Printed and bound by Jellyfish Print Solutions, Swanmore

To Mother,

without whom none of this would have been possible

TABLE OF CONTENTS

PART II – DECISIONS

PART III – REFLECTIONS

ACKNOWLEDGEMENTS

When completing a project such as this, there are always people to thank, and with good reason. In particular I must thank Marina, my dear mother, who makes everything so easy. Not only is she everything a mother should be, but every day she gives an inimitable personal life and warmth to Beth Shalom and its visitors.

My brother James is my partner in crime without whom nothing would happen. Not only does he give his time willingly to the cause, but he has sacrificed his love of medicine, and with it, his career, to be co-conspirator with me. Jim, it is appreciated enormously.

Yasmin puts up with my frequent absences. Thank you darling. As do my three lively – and ever energetic – children, Natalia, Stephanie and Aaron.

To everyone else who has helped directly or indirectly over the years in the creation of Beth Shalom, you know who you are. Thank you to all of you. Everything you have done is appreciated immensely.

To all those who put up with my irritating energy and see each deadline as a challenge rather than a chore, thank you.

And to all of you who recognise that the work of Beth Shalom has value and support us in achieving our aims, thank you. You are the ones who give this book the meaning I would like it to have.

INTRODUCTION

"But I don't understand, how exactly did you come to get so involved?"

"Could you spare me just a few moments to tell me how it all came about?"

"It really is something, but why in the middle of Sherwood Forest?"

Every day – yes, I mean every day – someone somewhere asks me to explain how it is that in the middle of rural Nottinghamshire, a family with a Christian background came to start Britain's first dedicated Holocaust memorial and education centre, Beth Shalom. It is a good question, and one that needs answering.

This book should go some way to answering some of those questions more fully than a conversation allows. It intends to give a glimpse into the origins, ethos and aims of the Beth Shalom Centre. As with any life-absorbing experience, there is always much more one could say, and so as not to risk being monotonous, I have tried to keep my comments and insights as brief as possible. I did not know quite how to do this without being somewhat autobiographical in style. If I had chosen any other format, it would have had to be more prosaic, poetic or academic, but I rather suspect my readers will really want to know just what motivated this project, what we did, why, and toward what end. That is what I have set out to explain and I hope it gives a clear picture.

Because of its content, this book is not just for reading, but also for sharing. I hope that it will inspire us all to continue our efforts to commemorate the victims of the Holocaust, and to create a world in which the potential for repetition of such inhumanity is greatly reduced.

This revised edition contains much of the original text, but in an expanded and updated version to reflect the latest developments at Beth Shalom.

Stephen D. Smith
June 2002

PART ONE
DISCOVERIES

C H A P T E R   O N E

TRIP TO JERUSALEM

I distinctly remember wanting to touch those huge stones. There was both the urge to feel the history and to mingle among the sounds of the prayers being offered there. It was probably the first time I had encountered history and tradition bound together like this, other than on our infrequent visits to cathedrals back in England. As I stood there, with the huge blocks towering above me, I could feel both their challenge and their power. It is difficult to describe how important that day was to become in my life, though of course I did not know it then.

I was just thirteen years old at the time. I had been brought up in a loving and caring home where Christianity had until that time played a central, if not the only, role. Mother, Father, James and I were standing at the back of the open square in Jerusalem where the Western Wall or *Kotel* is situated. We were frankly a little overawed, and certainly very excited at being there. Yet we did not really know quite what we were looking at, why it seemed so impressive or quite what to do once we were there. We approached the wall, my mother turning to the right to go to the ladies' section. We stood looking over the fence for some time at the comings and goings of Jewish men praying at the wall. It was Friday afternoon – *Erev Shabbat* – and to be honest we had no idea what was going on around us. We knew that Saturday was the Sabbath. We also knew that the Jewish festivals had begun the evening before, but did not realise that there was a long build-up to Friday night, and that the activity down at the wall was largely related to this.

The three of us obediently put on those paper *yarmulkes* that the man at the gate hands out as you try to enter without a head covering. Father, James and I walked up and stood by the wall, peering across to see if we could see mother over the *mehitza* which divided the men from the women. I remember looking at its deeply-riven surface, examining its texture, wondering if it had always been like that, or whether it had weathered over time. Close up, it no longer seemed, as it did from a distance, like an oversized garden wall with little ant-like people milling around its base. It was imposing, eternal and immovable. As I stood there, I tried to pray something, but did not quite know what to pray. I was intrigued by the bits of paper with prayers written on them – *kvetl'ch* – stuffed into the joints of the blocks. I was momentarily tempted to take one out to see what was written on it. Instead I found myself staring at the gnarled stone a few inches away from my nose with a question floating round my head. "How is it that we come to this beautiful city to learn something about the origins of our Christianity and yet, when we see a part of that, as Judaism is being practised here today, we don't know what is happening?" I queried further, "Why not? Aren't these Jewish people praying at the site of the Temple where Jesus of Nazareth came to pray as a Jew? Aren't they praying in the same language, the same prayers? If I consider myself a follower of that same Jesus, shouldn't I understand something of what is happening here?"

Actually I lie, of course. I was too young to formulate those particular questions in that particular way, but they indicate the essence of what I was thinking. As I look back and try to remember the sensation of standing there, can I say for certain that those would have been the questions to emerge from the confusing buzz in my young head if I had known how to ask them? I knew that I wanted to understand the connection between Judaism and Christianity, between them and me, between past and present. I knew that there was something missing in my knowledge. I knew that I had lots of questions and wanted to know the answers. What I do remember is this: I was so absorbed in what was happening, I didn't want to leave. I felt that hidden there, somewhere in that stone wall, was a dimension of my life that I had yet to explore. And I wanted to know more.

That was in March 1981. I was about to turn fourteen in April and James, my brother, was coming up to twelve years old. The family holiday to Israel was more of an adventure for us than anything else. It was a chance to explore the world in a new way, to discover new people and places. Unlike a lot of children these days who take flying for granted, this was the first time we had been on an aeroplane. Our previous forays abroad as a family had always been by car onto the European continent. This alone made the journey more memorable. Friends of my mother and father had parents living in Ramat Eshkol and so we arrived and spent the week with the Backhouses. Through their kind hospitality, operating out of their flat, we went out each day to explore the city.

It turns out that my parents had made a wise decision not to go on an organised 'Holy Land Tour'. Instead they chose to explore the sights and sounds of Israel with us on our own 'do-it-yourself tour'. They set out to find what was of greatest interest to us as a family, rather than being dragged around with a coachload of people, all 'doing the Holy Land' in eight days. We were there principally as a Christian family trying to learn about the Holy Land and the meaning of its history and culture for us. Like many of the hundreds of thousands of people who have clambered onto chartered flights at Gatwick airport, we expected to go there and return enriched, having discovered more about who we are and the origins of our religious tradition. We expected to have things confirmed, underscored, explained and clarified. There was in fact much about it that was enriching.

Having just finished the interminable round of Sunday School stories from the New Testament, I felt there was something captivating about standing on the site where the Feeding of the Five Thousand was said to have happened, or where John the Baptist is said to have baptised Jesus. However, we very quickly discovered a complex, diverse and challenging Israel, which we had not bargained for. Whatever sense we made of that complexity, I do distinctly remember feeling more and more inquisitive about the ancient history of Jerusalem and its meaning for the Jewish people.

We hired a caravan on the shores of Lake Kinneret and explored the region around the lake, going into the Golan during our second week. Much of our time was spent quietly by the lakeside. It was March and the tourist season was yet to get underway, and so we almost had the whole place to ourselves. From time to time, Mother would sit and talk to us as we threw stones into the lake. On one occasion she said to me that all over Israel, Jewish boys of my age had just completed their *bar mitzvah* and were now considered men in their communities. I was impressed by this. I guess I was a little envious that they had the opportunity to become recognised within their community so young. As we continued to plop stones into the water, she impressed upon us the importance of making the right personal choices as adults, of taking responsibility for our own actions, and being independent in our social, moral, religious and spiritual convictions. She talked about the need to know who you are, what you are doing and the importance of following your own convictions. She had always been the spiritual light in our home, even though Father was the religious professional. At the time, this seemed somewhat like a teenage lecture. Now on reflection, it is clear that those few moments of discussion contained words of wisdom that have remained with us ever since. Those few words of advice created the context in which James and I would make some of our more challenging decisions later in our lives.

In fact we had just started on a long and exciting journey of discovery, although of course we still did not know that then...

CHAPTER TWO

HOUSE OF PEACE

I was eleven years old when my parents decided to make a courageous career change. Until then, my father had been a minister
in the Methodist Church and my mother was a secondary school
Head of Department teaching religious education. I remember
quite distinctly the day that things changed. It was 4 March
1978. I had got up early that morning to go on a school trip to
Wembley to see England's schoolboys play the schoolboys of
France. Growing up in the North Nottinghamshire coal-mining
village of Ollerton, this was a big day in my life. The fact that
England lost did not seem to spoil the excitement of travelling to
London, and all the fun that went with it. By the time I came
home, I had an England hat and scarf and a France rosette with
Le Coq Sportif printed in the middle of it. My friend Adrian
Singleton's father came with us. He teased us all by supporting
France throughout, which made us all both hopping mad and
hilariously happy. Naturally, I returned home early that evening
bursting to tell my parents about my great adventure. I started
telling them about the huge stadium and about Adrian's father
buying a France rosette to goad us with, and of course showing
off my England scarf. However, I had hardly started when my
parents said they had something very important to discuss with
me.

We sat down on those rather rough, hard settees in the
lounge, the ones with the prickly fabric, and Mother carefully

explained that she and my father had decided they wanted to start a charitable trust and buy a house where they could make their work in the Christian Church more meaningful. They planned to create a house, like a small conference centre or place of retreat, where people could come to study, to learn or to be quiet and reflect. They explained that they felt it was one thing working in the Christian Church, but it was another living a Christian life, and they felt they could best fulfil this by serving society in a broader way.

Apparently, they wanted to find a more meaningful way of making the Christian message work in everyday life. My mother then went on to explain that they had very little money to achieve this goal and so it might not happen, but that she and my father were going to hand in their resignations at their respective places of work. They wanted my brother and I to make the decision with them as it would inevitably have a radical impact on our lives, and we should choose to do it together as a family, or not at all.

It is strange, but both James and I readily agreed to this plan, even though it seemed to entail the possibility of a move away from friends, school and all the things which give you security as young children. I remember being enormously impressed with their bravery, as this was clearly a risky thing to do. I don't remember too much about the following six months, except that my parents were searching for properties, looking worried from time to time and praying like crazy for funding for the project. There were several false dawns and as the year wore on, the chances of finding a place were getting slimmer. The clock was running down too, because the house we were living in was owned by their now previous employer, who had another minister coming to take over. There was talk of living on the streets – or worse, with grandma! Notwithstanding the humour, they were running a risk, but it was one they felt they had to take. Indeed, it was a chance they were convinced they should take. You learn a lot from that as an eleven-year-old, perched on the edge of your seat, pretending not to understand what is happening around you.

Finally, in the nick of time in August, they purchased a very old-looking, tumbledown farmhouse, not far away, in the middle of the countryside about a mile from the village of Laxton. It fitted their meagre budget of £25,000, but really the place was in need of a lot of attention by that time. It had started life as a late-Victorian farmhouse on Thoresby Estate, built for the then Lady Manvers. It had been occupied by the tenant farmer and workers until the developing age of mechanisation made its use redundant. And so, over a number of years, it had fallen into disrepair. Mother's colleagues and friends shook their heads in dismay as they heard she was moving into such a place with two young children. The roof had huge holes in it, water was running down the inside walls and the place had to be entirely re-wired, plumbed and virtually re-roofed before the winter set in.

I remember clearly the discussion that revolved around the naming of this new place. Various ideas were discussed that would appeal to what would be a largely Christian clientele. I remember that most, if not all, of the alternatives were Greek in derivation, chosen for their New Testament links. But one option developed which was Hebrew in origin: "*Shalom*... peace, or... why not house of peace?", went the conversation. Although both of my parents had studied theology at college, neither had learned Hebrew formally, but they knew sufficient to know that *Beth El* was 'House of God', so by deduction, *Beth Shalom* would probably mean 'House of Peace'. "*Beth Shalom*, yes, *Beth Shalom* seems good." And so, even though the vast majority of Christians coming to the place would not recognise what it meant, and with no other Hebrew in our lives, we moved into our *Beth Shalom*.

It was a strange existence really. Exciting, too. There was constant banging, hammering and the grinding of brick dust. Winter came, and predictably the house still had no central heating. I suppose as youngsters we saw it as a great adventure, but it really was quite cold. It happened to be the winter in which snowdrifts piled up high, and temperatures of -12 degrees centigrade were a common feature. Another little family had moved into the house too, and soon there were a couple of flats on the top floor of the building where we lived. Come springtime, the building began to operate – albeit somewhat primitively – as a centre for conferences, study and retreat. Over the next few years, a number of families from local churches became an increasing part of the centre's life, and it took on a life of its own.

There was something important and unusual about our upbringing at this point. We were being brought up as Christians in an entirely non-denominational or inter-denominational setting, in which faith formed a key part of our lives, but not the ritual of institutional Christianity that we had been used to up to that time. It meant that we had to rub shoulders with people who had different points of view, and learn to assimilate the variety of perspectives that existed. Faith became something to be worked out in practice. It was about kindness and goodness, about seeing the needs of others as a part of your own human responsibility; it was about education and learning to understand others; it was about making life worth living. I grew up believing that although there was evil in the world, people ultimately have the ability to be good.

And that is when we made our family visit to Israel, and a whole new chapter began to develop in our lives.

CHAPTER THREE

DISCOVERING THE JEWISH TRADITION

When we returned from our holiday in Israel, life continued pretty much as it had before. Mother and Father worked very hard. James and I toed the line, did our schoolwork and learned a lot about life from the comings and goings of the activities at Beth Shalom. As well as the conference work, people suffering from a range of personal problems would come and spend time at the centre. They would be cared for, counselled and supported by Mother, whose ability to support and look after souls lost in the mire of human existence knew no bounds. No two days were the same and so we experienced a life of colour and variety. Of course, we lived 'above the shop' and my parents did not draw a salary, so we never had anything but a very basic lifestyle and they worked twenty-four hours a day. They did what they did because they wanted to, and I discovered through their commitment that there is no greater reward than satisfaction at the outcome of one's labours. Through that day-in, day-out dedication to the cause of enriching human existence, I learned that to make the world a better place is an end in itself, and a worthy one too.

Aside from the daily routine, our visit to Israel had sparked an informal interest in Israel as a country, but more broadly, in the Jewish tradition, history, religion and culture. This didn't manifest itself in any particular way, except that we probably read a few more books, or watched a few more documentaries on the Jewish experience than would otherwise have been considered normal for the average Christian family living in the North Nottinghamshire coalfield. I remember shortly after our return, borrowing Chaim Potok's *The Chosen, The Promise* and *My Name is Asher Lev*. Somehow, I had managed to switch from the amazing fantasy world of J.R.R. Tolkien's *Lord of the Rings* to issues of Jewish identity in late twentieth century New York, and for some reason I found the latter far more fascinating.

I am not quite sure why I chose to sit for Religious Studies O-Level. Probably because I thought I could do it quite easily with my background, and also because Mother had been teaching it for years and had all the notes I would ever need. I took it a year earlier than my other O-Levels, along with English, and was very proud of my achievement. I hadn't considered studying Religious Studies beyond this, as I only really wanted to add it to the tally at the end of my school career. I duly left school at sixteen, as I had only one ambition ... to be a farm manager! I had spent every holiday driving tractors since the age of fourteen. I had my own little livestock business and was sure that if I applied myself, there was no reason why I couldn't become a farm manager. I enjoyed starting work enormously, but then when James was preparing to do his A-Levels, I realised that I should have done the same. I worked part-time, studied part-time, and yes, chose Religious Studies as one of my A-Level subjects. This time, the intention was more genuine. Since I was interested in the Jewish tradition, it seemed a good opportunity to further my knowledge more formally, and I chose Judaism and Christianity as my two subjects. The idea was to compare and contrast what I found and to get a sense of the underlying principles of the two religious traditions.

What I discovered was troubling. I found myself looking at

two religious traditions that claimed similar origins, and yet seemed to have little, if anything, in common in practice. Furthermore, the deliberate creation of a set of differentiated feasts, fasts and festivals began to look a little as though Christianity had subversively carved out an identity for itself as far removed from its original source as possible. It seemed wrong to claim to inherit all of the prophecies and revelations from Jewish faith and history and then to regard it as no longer viable. At this point I was not gaining this understanding through anything didactic. I was simply deducing that there appeared to be a constructive deficit in the relationship that was unhealthy. "How is it that I am studying two religions emanating from the same traditional sources, in the same places and at the same time, and yet reading their respective histories, it is as if the two had never met?" I found myself asking. It seemed that somewhere, the Christian world was not saying or admitting everything it should. In addition, it was clearly pushing Judaism out of the frame. This I found both disturbing and confusing.

By this time, I had made the decision that I wanted to study Christian Theology as an undergraduate degree, since I felt it was important to understand the origins of Christianity more clearly. This was very much against my better judgement: the fact that both my parents had studied theology seemed to give me every reason not to follow that path. That said, I was beginning to enjoy the enquiry. I started to think that if I were to study such a course, I would then be in a position to run some seminars at the centre on a variety of theological topics, which might benefit the visitors. I was also becoming increasingly curious about the genesis of Christianity, and I began to suspect that the vast majority of Christians understood little of its origins and development. I simply wanted to know more.

I registered as an external student at London's Birkbeck College and went down to London each year to do my exams. In the meantime I worked with my parents. As my father was taking a less active role at the centre, I spent more time working with my mother, studying whenever I could. Eventually, I set up and ran a couple of coffee shops in nearby towns which occupied much of my time. Study came second, but I was determined that I wanted to know more about this complex relationship.

I carefully chose my topics of interest to cover as much of both Jewish and early Christian history as possible. So for example, studying Early Israelite Religion was my means of understanding something of the beginnings of the Jewish tradition. Old Testament Studies was a way of seeing how that developed, particularly during the pre-exile and exile periods. Inter-Testamental Studies allowed me to explore the period out of which Christianity and Rabbinic Judaism were ultimately to emerge. New Testament Studies was compulsory, but nevertheless, I chose texts that dealt with issues of Jewish identity, as I tried to understand the new and developing doctrines of an increasingly Roman Church. Studying the Development of Jewish Literature taught me about the codification of the oral tradition in the Talmud and its constituent consequence for Rabbinic Judaism. Finally, Church History was my way of evaluating how the Church, particularly in its early years, sought to form its own identity as distinct from Judaism. It was as close as I could get to a degree in Jewish studies in a theology department which only offered one course with the word 'Jewish' in the title. And my tutors and examiners never even knew!

Out of this experience emerged a very disturbing discovery. I began to realise that the persecution of the Jews and the development of antisemitism were inseparably linked to the development and emergence of Christianity. I seriously did not know what to do with this finding. Nobody was teaching me or coaching me through this, and at first I was somewhat scared by it. I was scared that if I were to admit it, somehow my own Christian identity would be marred, or that it would be a blasphemy of some kind. I found Rosemary Radford Ruether's book, *Faith and Fratricide*, in the library, and read it with concern and a certain amount of trepidation. She describes in some detail the troubled relationship between Christianity and Judaism, and particularly the developing anti-Judaism, then the antisemitism of the emerging, then powerful Christian establishment. Then I was confused. "What happens if this is not the case and she is deliberately making this out to despoil the Christian image?" was the first thought to emanate from my disbelief at the treachery of Christianity toward Judaism. Before I left the library, my question had changed. "And what if what she says is true?" That seemed worse.

It took me several months, personally and professionally, to come to terms with what I was learning. The more I read, the more it confirmed the fact that indeed Christians had first distanced themselves from the normative practices of Judaism through the persistence of anti-Judaism in their earliest teachings onward.

Christianity then appeared to have used its political, social and economic power to isolate, discriminate against and persecute Jews, simply because they were Jews, from the fourth century right up to the present day. And then, just when I thought that this could not get any worse, I began to discover that my own 'philosemitic' soul was carrying the baggage of two thousand years of discrimination in the western world. The language of Christianity, for a start, with its persistent allusions to 'new' as opposed to 'old'; the use, abuse and de-contextualisation of texts within the Hebrew scriptures, used over and over again to justify the vilification of the Jews in the 'messianic' era; and, perhaps worst of all, the reworking of the message and words of Jesus of Nazareth, himself a practising Jew, in order to justify the removal of Christianity from the Jewish environment. The list was endless.

It was only at this point that I began to realise the importance of understanding and exploring the relationship between Jews and Christians in more detail. It was then that I decided to pursue my studies further and make it my concern to understand this relationship in the contemporary context.

CHAPTER FOUR

JIM AND I

It sounds as if all these discoveries were made and questions asked alone, but I am unintentionally deceiving you somewhat. You see, throughout the years of enquiry and slow realisation, it was a mutual, family interest, stemming from the first visit to Israel and the conversations that followed thereafter. Mother and I would discuss things because she was always interested. However, my other closest ally and friend was – and is – my brother, James. I would like to tell you a little about him, because without him this road of discovery would have been too lonely to travel.

James is two years my junior; young enough to push around when you are eight, but old enough always to have been my closest friend. That is the way it always was. I pretended to make all the decisions, but really he was the one with all the opinions, and it worked for us. We never fought. James was happy to have the opinions; I was happy to get things done.

While I was slowly working my way through my exams, he was already catching up on me, completing his medical degree just a year after I finished my undergraduate degree. This meant that intellectually we were coming of age at about the same time. The result was that we were able to spar on certain topics. As my medical knowledge was limited to O-Level Biology, I was not much fun on that front, and so we began to spend more time discussing, among other things, the issue of the Jewish-Christian relationship and the problem of antisemitism in the Christian tradition. James was studying in Leeds and I spent quite a lot of time at his house around exam times as I could gain access to libraries at Leeds University for revision.

We began reading the British Jewish press and realised that we knew nothing much about the life of the Jewish community in Britain, and started to take a little more interest. Soon enough we found a growing number of Jewish friends and our circle began to widen. We were taken to synagogue from time to time, attended lectures and started to discover a world within a world. It was fascinating, absorbing and interesting.

I began to wonder how to further my studies and how best to increase my knowledge of the Jewish-Christian relationship and its current dilemmas. I was looking for a topic that might make a suitable PhD subject and thought that to spend some time learning about a Jewish community in contemporary British society would provide an insight into the community. I wanted to know more about its workings and the issues that face Jews today, aside from the Jewish-Christian issue. My intention at that point was to study the history and development of the Jews of Leeds.

James and I went one evening to listen to Professor Geoffrey Wigoder, formerly a Leeds man, who had become better known as Editor-in-Chief of the *Encyclopaedia Judaica* and a representative on the Catholic-Jewish Liaison Committee. Professor Wigoder was speaking on the topic of 'Jewish-Christian Relations since the Second World War,' reflecting on what had happened in the relationship since the disaster of the Holocaust. His comments were enlightening and compelling, and demonstrated that the relationship still had much further to go. For some reason, his presence seemed too awesome for a direct approach that evening. Instead, I wrote to him in Jerusalem, explaining that it seemed there was much still to be done in this area (an understatement if there ever was one), and that James and I intended to dedicate some of our time and energies to engaging with this issue. His warm and encouraging response left us enthused to learn more.

In a bid to sound out the ground for my proposed thesis, I went to see the *sheliach* in Leeds, who suggested that before I got any further involved in a study of the British Jewish community, I should spend some time in Israel. He pointed out that understanding Israel was important to an understanding of the British Jewish community. Not knowing quite what a *sheliach* was, I didn't know that he was bound to suggest such a course of action, but nevertheless James and I decided to spend the summer in Israel. I was awaiting my exam results and thought it an ideal opportunity to spend a little time thinking about what to do next, meeting some people and learning some basic Hebrew. I signed up to the summer course at the Hebrew University. James, who had an elective period at university, chose to spend part of his time at Hadassah Hospital, at Ein Kerem, Jerusalem, and then a couple of weeks on the summer course. And so, in July 1991 we found ourselves back in Israel for what was to be another life-changing experience.

Chapter Five
Confronting The Holocaust

While we were in Israel, James and I decided to use our spare time as fully as possible. We had a hunch that this would not be our last visit. We also knew that even if work was to bring us back in the future, this was the time to see the sights and sounds of Israel and do everything that natives and regular visitors do not do. We went to the Israel Museum and the Diaspora Museum, around the walls of the old city and to the citadel. We walked up the Mount of Olives and visited the Temple Mount, we went to the Knesset and even Jerusalem Zoo! Whatever was on offer, we did it. However, there was one place that we wanted to visit that we considered a particularly solemn undertaking. This time we did not go as tourists, but with a sincere obligation to face and contemplate a particularly difficult part of the past. And so we made our way one hot July day to Yad Vashem, the Holocaust Memorial Centre in Jerusalem.

I seem to remember that we put the best part of a day aside to go there and try to understand a little more about the Holocaust, its history and meaning for the Jewish people. We already knew something about the Holocaust as our general interest in things Jewish had naturally attracted us to try and comprehend a little of what had happened. We had seen a number of films and documentaries and had read a few basic books. We had absorbed some of the fundamental facts and figures and would have been able to hold a reasonably informed conversation about the Holocaust. So we were not entirely ignorant. In spite of this, we had never really stopped to ask ourselves what the Holocaust might mean for us as individuals. It was one of those things we thought we knew about, but actually had never taken the time or trouble to confront properly.

That day at Yad Vashem we set out to try to understand the challenge of the Holocaust for us in a different way. Of course we were not doing this as Jews, because clearly that was not our background. We didn't go there to confront our own identity, knowing that had we been there, we too would have been marked as victims of genocide. Nor were we there as the children of survivors whose whole lives have been turned upside down by the dark cloud of personal trauma and tragedy. Nor were we there as second generation Germans who might have to live with the guilt and anger of a previous generation's evil. We were just there as ourselves, detached and unaffected, asking what this might mean to us as individuals who could legitimately claim that it had nothing to do with us. Our question was, quite simply, "What should the challenge of the Holocaust mean to us?"

I remember so distinctly walking around those darkened galleries. I don't remember seeing the perpetrators, but the faces of the victims remained with me. I don't remember absorbing what was done and how, but I registered clearly to whom it was done – and it made no sense at all. And then the questions started to boil inside me. Why? Why did they do it? How could they do it? At times I was angry, at times I was sad, but most of all I was simply confused.

We emerged into the bright sunlight and sat in the garden somewhere, overlooking the valley below, and began asking questions of ourselves. Confronting the Holocaust at a place like Yad Vashem is an immensely moving and emotional experience. It leaves one disorientated, in confused turmoil. There is both the sense of loss and of the overwhelming evil that would create such destruction. Somehow, the world did not seem the same place as the one we imagined just a couple of hours previously. But the overriding memory of that day is of the challenge it posed to us, as individuals, as professionals and as part of the human race.

Our first question was, "Why the Jews?" You see, we were not coming to this with no background knowledge at all. We knew something of the variety of Jewish life in Europe. We knew something of the richness of the tradition and culture of the Jewish communities in Eastern Europe. We were well aware that they had led a harmless, poor and often pious existence, with no interest in subverting the interests of any other group or society. The culture and contribution which Jews had been making to science and the arts for centuries was undeniable. Their tenacity in remaining a vital part of a largely hostile environment was as remarkable as it was productive. So, why them? It did not make sense.

Then there were questions around the roles of the perpetrators and bystanders. How was it that educated, civilised, cultured people could create such a monstrous state, in which the destruction of European Jewry could become such an integral aim? More troubling still was our concern that this was not just the ideological dream of a small clique of rabid antisemites. Every sector of German life, it appeared, had supported the aims of the Nazi regime and had consciously or subconsciously contributed to the success of the mass murder of the Jews of Europe.

We also thought about the mentality of evil that reduced the destruction of entire communities to a bureaucratic order. We now know from Heinrich Himmler's diaries that he was not just a bureaucrat behind a desk. We know that he travelled around the killing operations of Eastern Europe with avid interest. But behind him were an army of people who were just doing their jobs as they telegraphed the Eastern Front... and Jewish children died as a consequence. It's easy for me to say that they were antisemites and therefore outcasts of the civilised world. It's more difficult to admit that they were human just like me; that they did their PhDs, played the piano, visited the opera and enjoyed their skiing in the Alps; they went to church and said their prayers and told their children to be good. These people learned to heal, to invent and to communicate. They created laws, took pride in their education and dreamed of a perfect future. But the question for us that day was, "At what cost?"

As we extended our discussion, we found ourselves asking questions about the professions. Judges, who were trained to despatch justice, sent people to forced labour or to their deaths because of who they happened to be, or what they happened to believe. Teachers stood in front of their classes and taught race sciences and political propaganda week after week, many of them knowing that the 'knowledge' they bestowed upon their pupils was spurious and dangerous. Doctors, trained to heal the body and the mind, carried out the T4 euthanasia programme and sterilised tens of thousands of 'socially unacceptable' individuals. It was medical professionals who carried out the selections on the ramp at Birkenau and medical professionals who took 'research opportunities', experimenting on otherwise perfectly healthy individuals, killing them or maiming them for life. Clergy, charged with the Christian message of hope, forgiveness, love and goodness, incited their congregations to hatred or allowed them the liberty or passivity, and hence the guilt, of collusion. And did they know? Of course they did. But very often what you say you know is limited by what you are prepared to admit. Stunned by the realisation that this happened in the real world of real people, James and I began to ask how much of this had been confronted by our society, by our world and professions. "If, God forbid, we were given a second chance, how would we do next time? Have we learned anything? Have we progressed at all?" we found ourselves asking.

We were aware that the Holocaust was largely marginalised, but that there were some signs that it was increasingly becoming an issue for society. At that time, the War Crimes Bill was attempting to make its convoluted progress through the legislative process. The fact that Britain was considering the prosecution of Nazi war criminals at all was interesting, even if there appeared only a slim chance of securing convictions. The determination to put on record that such crimes should not go unpunished was as important as any trials that might follow. The House of Commons was passing the Bill, the House of Lords rejected it. The Bill became a moral and legal ping-pong ball, travelling back and forth between the Houses. Eventually Margaret Thatcher invoked the little-used Parliament Act to force the Bill onto the statute books. It was clear from this process that, for whatever reasons, some sectors of British society were more than willing to avoid a confrontation with the Nazi past, or even to cover it up.

At the same time, there was also discussion about study of the Holocaust becoming part of the educational national curriculum for England and Wales. Greville Janner MP was vociferously campaigning both for the War Crimes Bill and the inclusion of the Holocaust on the national curriculum, and he had started The Holocaust Educational Trust to lobby on behalf of these issues. As a result, the Holocaust was soon to be listed as a compulsory topic on the history curriculum for students in Key Stage 3 (11-14 year olds). So progress was being made behind the scenes, although James and I were not aware of this when we stood at Yad Vashem.

What we did know was that there were clearly areas where the Holocaust was not being addressed at all. As a medical student, James had just completed an introductory course in medical ethics. We could not understand why such a course, even taking into account its brevity, could not at least reference the Holocaust as a warning. Surely if the aim of such a course is to question the boundaries of modern medicine, and within that the role of personal and professional choice, some sense of what is right and wrong, and what is possible, have to be accounted for. The medical students of Berlin and Vienna of the 1920s did not train to maim, murder and kill. And yet some of these graduates went on to do just that. Why 45% of the medical profession were signed-up members of the Nazi Physicians League is complex to analyse. Not all by any means took part directly in harming human life. However, they did associate themselves with a regime which ultimately committed genocide in their name, as its members. Matters of choice are important. To serve one's career or an ideology of any kind at the expense of the life or dignity of any individual is to desert the cause of medicine. We understood that these happenings could not be ignored. James commented that "education is important at that level because if it did happen, it shows it can and therefore it might... Is that not warning enough?"

In an entirely different field, as a graduate theologian I was concerned about my total lack of understanding of the role of the Christian churches in the success of National Socialism as a political exercise, and by extension in the mass destruction of European Jewry. The persistence of antisemitism within the Christian tradition and connivance of Christianity with National Socialism seemed too coincidental to be ignored. I was wondering why nobody had told me that in July 1933 both Protestant and Catholic Churches could commit themselves to the framework of the National Socialist State, not desisting in that relationship for the full twelve years of Nazi domination. Of course there were lone voices of dissent. They, however, were not speaking on behalf of the Church, but in spite of it. "Where does that leave the Christian Church?" I found myself asking. "Can Christianity claim to have any credibility after such an unforgivable desertion of its christian cause?"

We were sitting in the Avenue of the Righteous at Yad Vashem, where thousands of non-Jewish individuals are remembered with gratitude for what they did in saving Jewish lives from otherwise certain death. There is no doubt that they were real heroes who defied the full force of National Socialism and took on the Nazis single-handedly. Of course they never would and never could defeat them alone. In fact that is not why they took action. They acted because they felt they should and could. Many of those individuals were practising Christians – many were not – and so it might lead one to conclude that because as Christians they carried out such wonderful acts of heroism, Christianity leads to altruism. Maybe their scarcity demonstrates that this is only likely in a small number of cases and may therefore have little to do with Christianity itself.

At the end of our visit to Yad Vashem, we decided that we must respond in some practical way to what we were seeing. We did not feel we could walk away from there and carry on with our normal lives as if nothing of consequence had happened. The Holocaust, it appeared, had huge consequences for us and for our generation. People have often asked us since, "How is it that millions of individuals go to Yad Vashem and are moved by what they see there, but very few actually react as you did? What was it that lay behind the kind of response you had?" These are important questions, and the answer probably lies not in our reaction to the atrocities themselves, but in the feeling of being let down by those who had subsequently failed to raise it with us. We felt that this was an issue that we should engage, and yet we knew that most of our peers would be totally disengaged from it. The Holocaust as an event in human history also flew directly in the face of the value system we had been brought up with; it railed against us in the most forceful of ways. Somehow we simply could not allow it to be ignored. It seemed too important for that.

We felt let down somewhat because we wanted to know how it was possible to go through school and university and even take an interest in things Jewish, without anyone at any point in our formal education saying to us, "Listen, this is the Holocaust; it is a tragedy for all time for the Jewish community, but it also matters to you." Although we knew something of the history of the Holocaust, in our mid-twenties we were discovering and confronting it for the first time as an issue which might be important for our own lives. Suddenly we were faced with huge questions but apparently nobody was armed with any answers. The propensity of otherwise good people to be extraordinarily evil; the nature of responsibility in society; the choices one makes, and the impact these have on the lives of others; the strength and weakness of democracy, and the importance of valuing human life: these and many other issues bombarded us.

On the other hand, our reaction was conditioned in part by the shattering of a somewhat idealistic belief in human goodness, in spite of the evil and suffering in the world. That is, I think until that point we believed that although there was evil in the world, good would always somehow triumph or at least pull through in the end. Here, clearly, evil had triumphed and there was very little goodness in sight. It turned our moral world upside down. Instead of hope, there was despair, instead of goodness there was despair. There was little that one could say redeemed any optimism in human endeavour because clearly the propensity for destruction was deeply embedded in what we refer to as western civilisation, and more likely in any civilisation.

I consider myself to be a creative person. That is, the appreciation of beautiful things, in particular the immense beauty of the natural world, is part of my enjoyment of life. My hobbies as a youngster were music, photography, writing, travel – the sorts of activities that allowed me to engage in creating, communicating and appreciating the world in which I found myself. My reaction to the Holocaust therefore was never conditioned by morbid fascination, but by a distinct revulsion at the wanton destruction of peace-loving, ordinary, yet beautiful people. It ran counter to my nature and I therefore wanted to confront it. It angered me, it saddened me, and it strengthened my resolve. Somehow, confronting the Holocaust meant finding ways of creating beauty for the future, in spite of the ugliness of the past. That is, I wanted to find out what had allowed the Holocaust to occur, and begin to confront whatever it was, because without such a confrontation, repetition was more likely, or so it seemed. On one level, becoming absorbed in the Holocaust was something I didn't want to do; that is, I had no inclination to do for its own sake. Knowing which camp was run by which commandant, on what budget, decided by which policy, was less important to me than establishing the broad principles that lay behind the catastrophe. Most importantly, I became involved because the Holocaust represented the opposite of everything I believed human societies should be.

And so the questions kept coming. "What of human nature, are we likely to repeat this kind of behaviour?" "Where does this leave issues such as ethics, politics and economics?" "Where does this leave the business community when businesses made prudent 'commercial decisions' and invested in their corporate future in the Third Reich?" "Were the thousands who were enslaved and worked to death a mere incidental outcome to this?" It seemed incomprehensible to think that this was not Egypt four millennia ago but Europe in the twentieth century.

We knew that the Holocaust was a tragedy of immense proportions for the Jewish community, the effects of which will take several generations to be realised. But we discovered something at Yad Vashem that day that we did not expect to encounter quite so strongly. For the first time, we understood that the Holocaust is not a Jewish issue at all. Somehow I had previously come to accept the fact that the Holocaust was an issue dealt with by Jews. As I understood it, Jewish people had generally contributed to making the films, books and documentaries I had seen or read. It is important that members of the Jewish community document and represent this as one of its most painful chapters, but our question was, "Where is everybody else?" Surely, Jews did not perpetuate antisemitism or perpetrate mass death; they suffered the consequences of antisemitism and the genocidal policies of others. Therefore the 'problem', whatever it is, seemed to lie fairly and squarely outside the Jewish community and was ingrained in West European civilisation somewhere. And so the responsibility to address and confront it needs to be taken up by a broad spectrum of people prepared to make that cause their

own. As we sat there in the heat of the Israeli summer, among the
mêlée of questions we were asking, one kept coming back. "Why
has no one done anything about this?"

We knew that across Europe there were few physical or educational spaces that offered a meaningful response to the tragedy
and challenge of the Holocaust. Former Nazi-occupied territo-
ries have hundreds of sites of destruction containing memorials
of some kind, but we suspected that they were there by default
rather than design. That is, they were being maintained because
they had to be, rather than because European society was taking
the issue of the Holocaust seriously. In some ways these sites had
become an excuse not to deal with the Holocaust, as they were an
unfortunate *fait accompli* on the landscape of European memory.
What we were looking for was a response which demonstrated
real care, rather than begrudging duty. If all that happened was a
maintenance programme for decaying sites, a number of road
signs and clusters of guides who could tell you about the history,
development and mechanics of say, Dachau, what would that contribute to an examination of European society in the wake of its
darkest hour?

In particular we were concerned about the ignorance of the
British public who seemed to suffer from what we saw as some
kind of 'victor's syndrome'. Britain played a crucial role as a
member of the Allied Forces who took on the might of the
German army and ultimately crushed and punished them and
restored democracy. But it appeared, perhaps because of that
final success, that we in Britain no longer felt the need to address
the Holocaust as a cause for concern, because it had not happened
here. Perhaps we felt a sense of moral high ground in which 'that'
débâcle was 'their' doing. The Second World War is an heroic
memory of struggle and determination against the odds, and for
those who partook and risked their lives, so it should be. It took
much heartache and not a little commitment to make possible the
ultimate defeat of Nazism, and it was service of immense importance. Still today the legends of the Battle of Britain, D-Day and

ultimately VE-Day make an Englishman's heart throb. Say 'Dig for Victory' and everyone knows exactly what you mean. However, if you were to refer to *Nacht und Nebel, Einsatzgruppen, Judenrat, Die Endlösung der jüdischen Frage*, and *Aktion*, the frightening terminology of Nazi occupation, the average Briton would look at you blankly. There are reasons, of course. There was the Cold War, with a Soviet threat which meant that British sensitivities toward its German adversaries had quickly to be turned into a relationship of constructive partnership, in which addressing the Holocaust was not helpful. Britain's position in Palestine and its relationship with the new state of Israel did not readily foster sympathy with Jewish suffering, as it was perceived to give too much leverage to Palestinian Jews in pursuit of their independence. And so somehow, the Holocaust was all but ignored in Britain for a very long time.

James and I felt that it was vitally important for British society be confronted with the meaning and challenge of the Holocaust, and that as a society we should ask ourselves what kind of issues we should be addressing, in order to be more certain that future generations are better informed than our own. As we left Yad Vashem that day, we decided to dedicate some of our time, energy and resources to assisting the British public in confronting the Holocaust and evaluating something of its meaning for their lives. We thought we might volunteer for an organisation or spend some time encouraging European governments to consider ways to engage the wider public in confronting the Holocaust. We just knew we wanted to do something and determined to go about it on our return to England.

That evening we arrived back at our temporary 'home' – our room at the Hebrew University on Har HaTsofim, Jerusalem – and were invited out by a couple who had become friends on the summer course. They were a very pleasant, amiable pair whose friendship was not hard to cultivate. He was Dutch and his wife German. As we sat in their little flat, eating supper, we explained that we had been at Yad Vashem that day, telling them how moved we had been and how much we wanted to find a way to respond to what we had seen there. In passing, during the conversation, I happened to ask whether they had been to Yad Vashem yet. To my surprise, the young woman replied in very negative tones that she had been to school in Germany, that she had done "that history" year after year and "did not intend to do it again". I was taken aback, possibly even insulted by the way in which she responded to something which was challenging the fundamentals of my existence. (Since that first encounter with German youth oversubscribed with Holocaust history, I have come to be more sympathetic: I now understand that the way in which Holocaust history was taught in Germany for many years was more likely to create barriers and resistance than to encourage openness and confrontation, a situation which has significantly changed in many instances in Germany today.) My reaction to this was to become even more determined to try and make people understand that this is not just another history, nor one we should be afraid to encounter; it is one we must be prepared to confront in all its troubling reality.

James and I very quickly found ready listeners in our parents who had come over to Israel for a short holiday during our stay there. We explained what we had experienced at Yad Vashem, and our concerns about apathy towards the Holocaust among many members of the British public. We discussed the need to raise this with our peers, and particularly with a Christian world which we perceived was still largely indifferent to the challenges posed by the Holocaust. We did not know quite what form such an undertaking should take, and were certainly not thinking of doing anything ourselves. The next day, we found ourselves discussing all this with an Israeli taxi driver, Yossi. Although the task of bringing this challenge to the wider public seemed somewhat daunting, Yossi's obvious enthusiasm and his view that such things should and could be undertaken by non-Jews, was our first indication that this was a history we could share in for the sake of our joint future. He doesn't know it, but the opportunity to share our concern with someone else who was prepared to listen, marked the very first step on our way.

It had been my practice since my early teens, whenever I found something meaningful, to try to write it down in poetry or find ways of expressing it in music. On returning from Yad Vashem, I created a series of poems and musical pieces to capture my reaction at the time. In those pieces I struggled with the broad issues of life and death, with responsibility, suffering and loss. I reflected on the callousness of the perpetrators and the dilemmas of the victims. It all came out in a flood of contemplation that spun around my head for weeks on end. Looking back, I am pleased I did that. Although I would not necessarily write the same pieces now, I know that the response I formulated at the time was considered and heartfelt. It seems important to me that any response to human tragedy should be made in as human a way as possible. That means thinking about the consequences for those caught up in it. It means putting yourself into their shoes and grappling with the dangers, struggling with the consequences. To respond to such a tragedy as an intellectual exercise with a duly-processed analysis is not enough, and indeed is arguably inappropriate if it is the only response. On the other hand, simply to react emotionally, without facing the inherent challenge it poses, is to escape the consequences in a different way. What I was trying to do was respond appropriately, by feeling the immense human tragedy and finding the right way to be challenged by it. And the challenge turned out to be bigger than I had ever imagined possible.

Among the many reflections of that time I wrote "My Little Light," a poem dedicated to the children of the ghettos. It is one that continues to have meaning for me.

My Little Light

My little light
You've shone through the darkness
You've shone through the blackness of the night
Don't cry my child,
Your light is still burning,
I haven't forgotten
Little flickering flame

When you stood on the ghetto corner,
Older than your years
So brave in the face of danger
You were just a child,
Holding back those tears

And when I look at your lonely faces,
When I see your eyes
I know your hearts were asking,
When can I be free?
Mama, who am I?

My little light
You've shone through the darkness
You've shone through the blackness of the night
Don't cry my child,
Your light is still burning,
I haven't forgotten,
Little flickering flame.

CHAPTER SIX

WHERE MEMORIES MEET

I was talking to one or two Holocaust survivors, explaining the interest James and I had in the Holocaust and that we really wanted to know more. They were very encouraging and suggested I keep learning. But one of them suggested that before going much further, we should take a trip to Poland to see what had happened, to whom, where and how. And so, in January 1992, my parents, James and I took the car and made our way to Poland.

Our route was not direct though. We started in Germany, driving down to Munich, where we spent the day. We then travelled on to Prague where we visited, albeit briefly, the Jewish quarter and cemetery, and of course the much visited *Altneu Shul*. The impression of those cobbled streets, old houses of prayer and the thousands of lonely graves will remain etched in my memory. It was that sense of Jewish life where there is no Jewish life. As in history, where the traces of the past are a remnant of a destroyed civilisation, it was not what we saw, but what was missing that most embedded itself in my conscience. They were just beginning to paint the names of the deportees on the wall of the Pinkas Synagogue, where now 80,000 names of Jews of Bohemia and Moravia are permanently inscribed. A young woman sat atop the scaffolding, painstakingly painting one name after another. It seemed tedious, until I reminded myself that every name was a life – and that in most cases, that one moment of inscription would be the only memorial they would ever have. Each name was like a funeral, fifty years late.

From there we headed into southern Poland and on to Krakow. When discussing the importance of visiting Poland, one of my survivor friends had commented that the country was like a large Jewish cemetery. The fact that the majority of the Jewish population was wiped out during its Nazi occupation, and that hundreds of thousands of Jews were brought there from right across the European continent for the sole purpose of killing them, makes it a place of very great tragedy in the whole of human history. However, we quickly discovered that Poland is not a Jewish cemetery at all.

I remember standing at the end of the ramp at Birkenau, where some one million Jewish men, women and children had been unloaded before they were murdered, and realising that although this was their final resting place, it was hardly a cemetery. At a cemetery you see the individual graves of individual people. There are names, dates of birth and death and each has a headstone bearing some personal symbol or epitaph in honour of that loved one. In a cemetery there is ritual, there is family and community; there is dignity and love. As I looked around me in the silence, I imagined the tired and dirty deportees arriving at this, their final destination. Within hours of arriving, they were stripped, gassed and burned, and everything they had brought with them was looted by their murderers. I went through the Jewish rites of death and mourning in my mind and soon realised that every rite, as practised in the Jewish religion, had been desecrated there.

Although in life many of us do not associate so closely with our respective religious communities, in death we are buried by our co-religionists, as co-religionists, and then lie next to them as a part of that community and its history. Whether the individuals who had ended their lives at Birkenau were religious or secular, the vast majority would ordinarily have been buried according to Jewish tradition, in Jewish cemeteries. I looked around me. "Where are the *matzevot*? Where are the names, the dates of birth and of death? Where are the individuals, the families, the communities, the dignity and love for the deceased?" I found myself asking. They were not there.

The next day, we spent some time travelling around the Polish countryside, and en route we passed through many little towns and villages. Knowing that before the war the Polish Jewish population represented over ten percent of the population, we had a little guidebook that told us something about the Jewish communities that had existed in the region. It didn't take long to realise that in each of those towns and villages there was no visible Jewish presence of any kind. The synagogues are gone, or perform another function, the schools are gone, the *yeshivot* are gone, along with the *mikvot*, the *kosher* bakers and butchers, the youth movements, the Communists and the labour Zionists. All are gone and will never return. The last remnants of these once thriving communities are found in the dishevelled, unkempt and at times vandalised cemeteries scattered across the countryside. We found ourselves looking for something that was no longer there.

This fact was even more profoundly impressed upon me on a subsequent trip to Belzec. It was toward the end of winter; some two feet of snow lay on the ground and had been building up over about a two-week period. I was going to Belzec because I knew that over 600,000 Jews had been murdered there. I was not ready, however, for the 'memorial' I was to find: a small, untidy piece of scrubland with a fence that had clearly not been maintained, and a square concrete monument that managed to avoid informing visitors that the victims of Belzec were Jews. What struck me most of all when we arrived was that although there were two feet of snow, not so much as a single set of footprints was to be found in it. No one had even entered that site for over two weeks.

At Belzec that day, I realised that the Holocaust was not only about the mass murder of European Jewry, but also an attempt to wipe out even the memory of the existence of those individuals and communities. On that day I realised just how successful the Holocaust had been. I had always consoled myself with the fact that it was not totally in vain, that the Jewish community had managed to revive itself, that lessons had been learned, that Israel now existed and a future could be built. That day I realised that it was all in vain. Nothing good comes out of the Holocaust. Nothing good at all. If anything is salvaged, it is not because of the Holocaust, but in spite of it. This turned upside down a principle that I had held, that out of bad things good can come; the kind of naïve optimism or fatalism that many hold. This scotched that idea once and for all. Out of bad things, bad things come, and anything good that emerges from it merely helps us to continue, but does not reverse the effect of the evil or undo the damage. The Holocaust was a waste of life, period. No, it was the desecration of life, the trampling of life, the humiliation, degradation, wanton destruction of people for the sake of destroying them. It was taking a child and shooting him through the heart. It was taking a man and making him fear every moment of every day, until he was thrown into the abyss. It was taking a mother and destroying her in front of her children, or worse destroying her children in front of her. It was taking the dignified and turning them into animals. There is nothing, absolutely nothing good about any of that.

It was then that I knew for certain that far more is lost than can ever be recovered. That among those hundreds of thousands of people were talents and skills, homes and institutions, learning and creativity, and that it all lay in a heap under the soil beneath my feet, either unrealised or destroyed in the carnage. It was then that I understood that far, far more is forgotten than can be remembered. Belzec is arguably one of the most significant historical sites anywhere on the European continent. Since my first visit there, the estimated number of victims of Belzec has risen from 650,000 to 800,000, all murdered in the space of ten months in 1942. There is no indication on the memorial of who those people were, where they came from, what family they left behind – if any at all. There is just a space where their anonymous remains lie. Only two people are said to have survived Belzec. The tragedy of this is that hardly a single person in Britain could even tell you what happened there.

On another occasion I had the privilege to be in Poland for two weeks with Dr Jonathan Webber of Oxford University, who was running a European Union Tempus programme, bringing together English, German and Polish students to confront the Holocaust, its history and consequences. This was also a seminal experience for me, not least because the mix of students was such that simply being able to talk together about the Holocaust in a meaningful way revealed just how differently we have come to perceive this history. Strangely, the same history which took place in the same places, had a different meaning to each of those on the trip. For some it was painful and personal, for others distant and less important. In talking to the participants, I began to realise that there is not a single version of the Holocaust, that we all overlay it with our own interpretations and contexts, and that I would always need to be careful not to read it in the way that suited me, but always to listen to what others had to say.

But the most important part of that particular visit for me was spending a whole week in the towns, villages, cemeteries and synagogues of once-thriving communities, and beginning to understand further just how much had been destroyed. We went to Tarnow, to Nowy Sacz, and to Bobowa, as well as to a host of little places with long and significant Jewish histories. It was moving to touch so much Jewish culture in such a short space of time. It was tragic to do so in the void of their absence. Jonathan had an amazing ability to be able to sniff out and explain in detail old synagogues, cemeteries, inscriptions on walls, *mezuzot* in doorways, *sukkot* on rooftops. At Dabrowa Tarnowska, I remember wandering around the grand old crumbling synagogue, its mural of the Twelve Tribes of Israel still clinging to plaster which was about to peel from the rotting walls. There in that little town, the community had been large enough, proud enough, to develop that wonderful building. They had designed it, built it, painted it, prayed in it. And now it was empty, a relic of a vanished civilisation. We wandered around the corner to the cemetery where we were met by the last surviving Jew of the community there. I don't even remember his name, but recollect so clearly standing watching as he talked, realising that when this old man was gone, there really would be nothing except the disintegrating synagogue.

I also began to understand more clearly how our representations of the past can either reveal or conceal the past. These forgotten places of the Holocaust were concealed by layers of forgetfulness, which seemed to add insult to its fatally injurious nature in Poland. Jonathan confined us to Galicia. We hardly ventured more than an hour or two away from Krakow, and yet day after day we picked among the ruins of destruction and saw only the shadows of a former world. When I looked at the small area of the map we had covered, calculating just how much destruction we had seen and how little was left, then scanned the whole of the European continent where the net result had been so similar in so many places, it became even harder to comprehend. My hopes that I would begin to understand this tragedy were becoming less and less likely with everything I saw and learned.

I think that on that occasion as never before, I also encountered the despair of the Holocaust in a different way. I remember in particular our visit to Tarnow and more particularly to Zbylitowska Gora, a small hamlet several kilometres away. There was a substantial ghetto in Tarnow: in 1942 it housed some 40,000 Jewish people. One day, some 6,000 Jews were taken from the ghetto, marched the several kilometres to Zbylitowska Gora and murdered in a small woodland on 11 June 1942. The beauty mixed with anguish there was overwhelming. The trees were majestic and quiet, allowing sunlight to filter down to the mass graves below their towering canopy. There was a low fence approximately demarcating the positions of the graves. On one of them, there was a plaque dedicated to the 800 Jewish children murdered there that day. This left me in a blinding despair I will never forget. "How could such innocent life be wasted? Who were these children? Does anyone know? Does anyone care?" Somehow, the 800 children of Zbylitowska Gora were helping me make sense both of the scale and intimacy of death in a way that neither Birkenau nor Belzec could. In those places of such huge scale, people are very quickly consumed by statistics and symbolism. It is hard to struggle against the tide of mass death, because the whole intent was to depersonalise and obfuscate the victims through the sheer numbers of their victimhood. At Zbylitowska Gora, I knew I was looking at the grave of the generation of Tarnow's Jews who should be leading the community now. It was the grandparents of today, buried in a hole of yesterday's madness. These children would have been around the same age as my parents, and they had been tossed aside because of who they were. As the numbers became smaller and the communities that had once existed came more into focus, I began to think that I finally understood something. Or at least, I was now beginning to realise what the consequences of the Holocaust really were. This didn't make things any easier, but it began to give a greater sense of direction to our own endeavours.

We also visited a Jewish cemetery in Nowy Sacz. In the middle of the largely deserted landscape, there is a small *ohel* in which members of the Halberstam Hasidic dynasty are buried. The *tzadikim* buried there would long since have been forgotten, had members of the family and their followers not emigrated before the Nazi occupation. Today their followers make the journey back to Nowy Sacz to remember their founders. It was sunset when we arrived there and in the half light of the *ohel*, as we peered in, we could see a little *yizkor* candle flickering. It was apparent that someone had made the journey there to remember the *rebbe*, because his life, teaching and wisdom still had meaning in their lives today. His followers would light their candle, say their prayers and return to their homes, wherever they may be. I thought about the forgotten victims of Belzec and the anonymous children of Zbylitowska Gora, and realised that no one visited them because they were truly forgotten, without a name, identity – a life to remember them by. It was then that I understood that it is the duty of anyone – or perhaps everyone – to make time to reflect and remember them, because we are the only memory they have.

On returning home to England, I couldn't see through the pain of the loss. I couldn't escape the screams that must have punctured streets and houses, synagogues and barracks alike. Nor could I escape the silence; the silence of inner anguish, of inevitability, of knowing and not admitting; the silence of empty space, of relics, of mass graves; the silence of not listening, not speaking, not responding; the silence of silence, the noise of silencing, the silence of the pleading victims. I couldn't get out of my head that the world had been broken, shattered by the Holocaust. It was a breakage of such force that I was certain it could never be mended.

PART TWO
DECISIONS

Above: Beth Shalom, 1978.
Right: Jim and I together in Israel, 1991.
Below: Visiting Yad Vashem, 1991

Mother, Jim and I together in Israel, 1991.

Construction work begins in the gardens at the centre as I get to grips with driving the JCB, 1992

Above: The memorial hall under construction, 1992.

Left: The roof goes on, 1993.

Below: A maturing garden surrounds the finished memorial hall, 1998.

Main Photo: Beth Shalom, seen through the main entrance gates.

Inset: The Gateway of the Righteous, set in the memorial gardens.

The Memorial Gardens: a place of peace in spite of the suffering it concerns.

The Memorial Rose Gardens: a significant and poignant part of the centre, where many people have planted roses for lost families, alongside those dedicated by school groups and civic dignitaries.

*Left: Jewish Refugee
Lisa Vincent talks with
students in the hall at
Beth Shalom.*

*Below: James fits an
image in the camp room
of the exhibition.*

*Bottom: In the
memorial exhibition;
more than just photos
and suitcases, yet these
provide a means to
visualise the
environments with
which it deals.*

Abandoned: A sculpture by survivor Naomi Blake.

Above: Members of a group relaxing on the patio over tea.

Left: Mother with her customary greeting.

Right: Professor Yehuda Bauer, then Research Director at Yad Vashem, delivers a keynote lecture in the Memorial Hall, September 1997.

Below: School pupils listening to a survivor relating their experiences in the Memorial Hall.

C H A P T E R   S E V E N

MAKING MEMORY

What James and I had now established was that whatever we were going to do in response to our learning about the Holocaust, it should be done foremost in remembrance of those forgotten individuals. But still we had no real idea how to go about this. Clearly we were in no position to name the victims of Belzec or Zbylitowska Gora or the hundreds of other sites strewn around the European landscape. We began to wonder, "What kind of place should exist? Where? To say what? Run by whom? And toward what end?" None of this was abundantly clear, other than the fact that someone should do something soon.

In the meantime I had taken a year out, prior to starting my doctoral thesis. I wanted to find a topic I felt more comfortable with, and also to spend some additional time doing further fundamental learning in Jewish studies. I spent a year at the Oxford Centre for Jewish Studies on Professor David Patterson's one year graduate programme, and this turned out to be an important year. Not only did I have all the hours of the day for reading and attending some wonderful courses, but I also found the time to think and reflect more than I would otherwise have done.

One Sunday evening, travelling back to Oxford from home, I was becoming a little frustrated. It was clear that what was needed was some kind of museum, memorial and education centre in the UK, a place that could confront British society with its own negligence and pose important questions which until that time were still studiously avoided. I was thinking about how a site might be found and government be persuaded to assist in funding such a project, how much it might cost, and where the team would come from to create it. More importantly, I wondered where several million pounds might come from to buy a site, construct a building and service an institution in London. And I realised that it was not going to happen. Not then, anyway.

I needed to talk to James. It was clear that something needed doing soon, because time was passing by and it seemed that such a project could not wait forever. At the same time, whatever else this project was, it should be set in a place worthy of its purpose. It should be a place of reflection and dignity, a place for learning and confrontation with the past. I then realised that I was probably expecting everybody else to do something about this, but then asked myself what might we ourselves be prepared to do? As if someone had turned on the light, suddenly everything became very clear. Beth Shalom was the obvious place to do something. I couldn't wait to talk to James, and of course, we would have to sit down and talk with Mother.

The initial idea was very modest. We talked it through together and felt that a project on the Holocaust with a number of rooms for a library and some pictures on a wall to serve as some kind of exhibit would probably be the best we could manage. At least that way we could ensure that visitors to the centre, and local schools and universities, would have the opportunity to come and be confronted by a small but meaningful place, and discuss their reactions to it. It would mean that we would be making some kind of contribution, rather than worrying about the fact that nothing was available in the UK.

It soon became clear, however, that a room with a few pictures on the wall was not going to be adequate, and so we considered how to create a broader programme within the facilities available to us. For some time, Mother had been planning an extension of the property and so we thought about utilising some of those spaces and also developing new ones. The new building was to incorporate two levels, one subterranean, the other an open hall. We had felt that the new building could somehow be a fusion of Christian and Jewish concepts and so we took early church and synagogue designs which often deployed polygons – usually octagonal – and created a sacred space for quiet and reflection. This was not an attempt to create a religious space per se, but a space that would engender contemplation and be reflective in nature. The plans to develop the project began to take place. We had determined early on that there was a need for non-Jews to make a more effective response to the Holocaust. Perhaps by making this contribution, things would begin to fit into place and we could give the signal that this was of concern to everyone.

Wanting to do something to commemorate the destroyed Jews of Europe is one thing; having the ability to do so is another. We had little knowledge and no experience, so it was clear that we would have to do some learning fairly promptly. Without wasting time, we began to extend our own study, both formally and informally. We became engrossed in research and reading, we went on courses to Yad Vashem, further trips to Europe and the USA and met with as many people who were running Holocaust centres as we could find. We also began to meet and talk with survivors, as well as sitting down to discuss with educators and curators. I seem to remember going to every conference anywhere that had the word Holocaust in its title. The result was a steep learning curve, absorbing as much experience as possible, as quickly as we could.

But there were also some fundamental questions we needed to address. We felt it was extremely important that whatever we chose to do should be seen as coming from outside the Jewish community. We knew that it was time for the world in general – and the Christian community in particular – to make a serious effort to face a situation which could not have occurred without the connivance of the environment it had created. As we thought about this, it quickly became apparent that we might not have the right to do such a thing. The Holocaust is a matter which is very close to the hearts of the Jewish community, in particular to survivors and their families. What right had we to start creating memorial spaces and educational programmes? What would happen if the Jewish community refused to accept the intentions of our effort and misunderstood what we set out to achieve?

We struggled with this issue for some time, but reached the conclusion that Beth Shalom should come from outside the Jewish community for a number of reasons. Firstly, the survivors had been badly let down for almost fifty years since the Holocaust was all but ignored by the western world. Many had wanted to speak about their experiences, but had no one to talk to in the lonely years following their ordeal. Today we often suggest that survivors were silent. In actual fact they were silenced. We felt it was important, if only for their sake, that Beth Shalom should clearly state that there were people outside the Jewish community prepared to take this on as their issue, to listen to those experiences and to deal with them honestly. We hoped, in so doing, not to remove the burden, but at least to make it a little easier to bear. Secondly, we felt that other non-Jews should see this as their issue too, and take some encouragement from our own commitment to this work. It was all too easy for non-Jews, particularly in Britain, to feel sympathetic to the issue without it posing any real challenge to their lives, convictions or actions. The Holocaust did not take place on British soil and therefore is not as embedded on the landscape here as it is on continental Europe. That is clearly to our advantage, except where it becomes the reason for detachment. We wanted to make the experience of the Holocaust less distant; to somehow find links and connections that would make people begin to connect themselves more readily to its reality.

Commemoration is naturally incumbent on those upon whose family lives the personal tragedy of the Holocaust casts a shadow. But we realised that to leave the survivors, their families and the Jewish community to fulfil this duty alone was to desert the cause of humanity. We began to see our role as fulfilling a duty of some kind. It seemed there was a duty to provide com-memorative memorial spaces within the context of British society for Britons to participate in, should they so desire. The Holocaust was not about the suffering of the Jews alone, but about the suffering of humanity, as experienced by the Jews of Europe. To avoid the role of remembrance was to fail at a very basic level in respect of our duty as fellow members of the human race. The fact that Jews were murdered on Christian soil was even worse, and therefore the imperative to fulfil that duty was even greater. We felt a duty to commemorate the Jews of Europe, not as someone else's suffering, but as part of that in which we share as human beings. That said, it was not an attempt to dejudaize the Jews, to sanitise them of their Jewish identity in the cause of humanity. On the contrary, Jews died because they were Jews. That was the reason they needed to be commemorated.

I am often reminded of the Passover Haggadah, where each year Jewish families recite the ancient story of the escape from Egypt. What amazes me each year when I hear those words, is that any Jew sitting around the table is reminded of his or her identity when told in no uncertain terms to remember that it was 'I' not 'them' who came out of Egypt. In so saying, Jews commit themselves to their Jewish identity, as they reflect upon what their ancestors endured. Of course, they do not actually relive those precise circumstances, but the collective memory of the escape from Egypt is a memory which brings people together in communal identity. In a similar way, to remember the Holocaust is not only to remember that something happened in history, but also to identify with those who went through it. This is not to suggest considering oneself a victim per se, but by coming alongside those for whom the memory is very real, to include oneself in their community of memory, rather than observe it from the outside.

This duty is not about the documentation of history – as important as that is – but about the way in which we remember the suffering of those who became the victims of another's evil.

The duty is not limited by creed or colour or personal experience, but by the sense of injustice and the cause of humanity, which simultaneously recognises that those potential victims suffered because, and only because, they were Jews. Conversely, not to remember the millions, for whom otherwise there would be no memory, is consciously to commit them to oblivion, and to present Hitler and his accomplices with their final victory. If we do not wish Hitler to have that victory, then the commitment to remember is a key component for the future.

In addition to the duty, which I encapsulate as remembrance, there is also a responsibility which encompasses the need to stimulate education, research and discourse. At the first confrontation, I was terribly stricken by the events of the Holocaust. However, I did not feel personally guilty about what happened: how could I? It was in the past and I was not there. However, I did – and do – feel a tremendous sense of responsibility: one of knowing that while the events are in the past and cannot be reversed, society should nevertheless know about and be challenged by them. The responsibility is principally toward those who otherwise might not know or make the personal effort to confront the reality of how serious this was – and is. To achieve this, disseminating what we know as widely as possible is crucial to its success. The responsibility is also principally focussed on telling a generation too young to remember, too distant to associate, too sheltered to appreciate its significance. It is the responsibility to ensure that one by one, we incorporate a wider group of people who understand the gravity of the Holocaust's consequences and formulate their response to it.

The Holocaust did not take place in another time and another place. It took place in the 'here and now' of human interaction, within the world of real people. It was therefore not an extraordinary event, but an ordinary event with extraordinarily tragic and disturbing consequences. For understandable reasons, we may have come to describe the Holocaust as an event virtually outside of human history, stimulated by our own desire to try and explain the extraordinary nature of what happened. Even the terms we use to describe it create a new language. The word Holocaust, for a start, the Hebrew variant *Sho'ah*, Planet Auschwitz, *L'univers concentrationnaire*, The Tremendum, are all terms used to describe an event which ruptures history by placing it outside the norms of linguistic usage. There is of course very good reason for this. How do you describe a gas chamber full of two thousand mangled bodies, which until a few hours previously had been mothers and fathers, brothers and sisters, doctors, lawyers, rabbis, writers, poets, footballers, actors, musicians and scientists? How do you convey, in 'ordinary' terms, pits full of burning corpses? What about the children, the wise old people who should have graced our society today, who were thrown alive into the flames? Where do you find the words?

Our responsibility though is not to lose sight of the fact that this happened through a gradual, step by step process and was carried out by individuals within the normal referents of human existence. Birkenau, Treblinka, Belzec, Sobibor, Chelmno and Majdanek are not on another planet. They existed in the here and now, then. Even in the muddled confusion of the time, when you read the harrowing stories of what happened inside the fences of Birkenau or the barracks of Auschwitz or the work *kommandos* of Majdanek, do not think for a moment that the whole world turned into a black and white movie. Inside the fences, red was still red and the sun was still in the sky. Outside the fences, the world carried on spinning and people lived their lives, notwithstanding the pressures of war. When the Nazis left 'work', they smoked their lights, drank their brandy and talked of their day at the 'office'. They knew what they were doing, and they did it from day to day. Of course they had created quite unprecedented circumstances in European history, but it was all carried out with deliberation. The conditions that we understand to be beyond imagination – which were indeed so for those who became victims – were created and controlled by people who chose to do so. The responsibility therefore extends to ensuring that such choices, such steps, are never again made.

Recognising the duty of remembrance and the responsibility of education was just the first step; fulfilling it was another operation altogether. The initial problem was how to create a suitable memorial space in the middle of a field, in the middle of North Nottinghamshire. We were attempting to commemorate the destruction of the Jews of Europe two generations previously, a thousand miles away, with no sizeable Jewish community in sight. How would one connect it to the landscape and the society in which it occurred? We felt that a monument would not be the most appropriate or fitting means of fulfilling that duty. This was partly because monuments tend to be more meaningful when linked to historical sites or publicly designated spaces, where in actual fact they often say more about the collective memory than they do about the events themselves. It was also partly because we did not want to create a passive piece of artistic representation which would be symbolic to the generation that went through the war, but would eventually lose its significance for future generations. Put more succinctly, we felt it more important to contribute to the education of a future generation than to create something emotionally or culturally satisfying for the present one. In this regard we spent time thinking about how to create the kind of spaces in which we could bring together people of all backgrounds and persuasions to confront the meaning of the Holocaust for history and for their own future.

After due reflection, we decided to create a 'memorial environment' in which our principal activity would be education. We felt that we should not enforce any single perspective on the Holocaust, but rather present some basic facts and act as facilitators to bring together people from across the spectrum of British society to confront the evil of the Holocaust and its consequences. In this respect, Beth Shalom was to be a 'house of peace' where we would provide a place of peaceful memorial in remembrance of the victims, and where we could also work together toward peaceful coexistence within our world. This was not the application of some idealistic 'peacenikism', but an attempt to find a meaningful way of contributing to the discourse on the universal values of human existence.

Although Beth Shalom was to emanate from what was originally an institution with Christian links, we also felt it was important for several reasons that our activities should avoid a Christian reading of the Holocaust.

Firstly, to impose a specifically Christian angle on the Holocaust would restrict its significance, its audience and effectiveness. Imposing a Christian reading would limit its message, predicate its outcomes, overly complicating agendas – and anyway we were finding our own Christian reading of history being challenged by the Holocaust, not vice versa. Even if we had been attempting a Christian interpretation of the Holocaust, it is clear that the Holocaust cannot be read in the context of Christianity (unless of course it is in examining the role of Christianity at the time), but Christianity needs to be read in the context of the Holocaust.

Secondly, we felt that the relationship between the visitors and the institution should be reciprocal. We hoped that the visitors would teach us and shape the project through their reactions, feelings, learning and research. To claim expertise in the Holocaust would be a fallacy, and we felt it would be limiting and trivialising to create a prescribed learning experience, where visitors are told that 'the lesson of the Holocaust is....' Even now, ten years on, I don't profess to know what the lessons of the Holocaust are, and the moment I think I do, I believe I will have lost the ability to learn, and therefore the ability to be effective. What we envisaged was a project that could confront attitudes, but one that could also be confronted by those who knew more than we did. If Beth Shalom was to be a genuine response to the Holocaust, it would be a place where that response would be shaped and honed by many new and difficult challenges, and by people from all walks of life who would benefit from what was there, but would also benefit the institution.

Thirdly we felt that Beth Shalom should be interdisciplinary since dealing with the Holocaust is, by necessity, interdisciplinary. Even if you were interested in evaluating theological responses to the Holocaust, how can you know this without first studying the history as history? How can you find out without research facilities? How will you understand the abandonment the Jews felt without reading the literature, filming the survivors, or investigating the theological reactions across a spectrum of thought before and after the outbreak of war? How can you understand the interpretations of theologians without reading the literature and documents that have emerged in the fifty years since? In other words, even to begin on any topic related to this (or any other discipline), you have to enter an interdisciplinary world of learning and enquiry, and we knew we had to provide the basics for anyone wishing to start that journey.

Having decided what we wanted to achieve, James and I felt it was of paramount importance to know what had been done in other places, and to develop our own learning skills. Our first port of call was back in Israel where we spent time at Yad Vashem. We both took part in the three-week intensive Graduate Institute programme there. James followed the summer course and due to constraints on my time, I followed later and did the winter course. While in Israel we spent much time in the archives, the pedagogical resource centre and the library at Yad Vashem. We travelled to Beit Lohamei Haghetaot (the Ghetto Fighters' Kibbutz), near Naharia, where there is a very fine museum and memorial. It was a particularly enriching experience to learn with young people like ourselves, as well as with more mature adults seeking to extend their own learning, and of course to do so with people from all walks of life and cultural backgrounds. At Yad Vashem the delicate balance of national memorial, museum, education centre and research institute is revealing in itself. Obviously, the development of those organisations demonstrated the need to fulfil the various roles through the creation of an institution that would be meaningful to Israeli society, to Jews around the world and to the vast range of non-Jewish visitors who flock there every year.

Immediately after my few weeks in Israel, I drove through Europe with a couple of graduates from the seminar, stopping at many sites, former camps and memorials: Bergen Belsen, Berlin, Poznan, Chelmno, Warsaw, Lodz, Treblinka, Lublin, Majdanek, Belzec, Krakow, Auschwitz, Birkenau, Gross Rosen, Terezin, Prague and Dachau. In each case I spent time evaluating the ways in which the history had been written and confronted. There were many surprises, too. Up to this point, I was unaware of the lengths to which governments, particularly in the Eastern Bloc, had gone to obfuscate the memory of the destruction of the Jews of Europe. Time after time, memorials failed to mention who the victims were, or prominence was given to general memorials, or even specifically Christian memorials which by exclusion denied the suffering of the Jews during the Holocaust. I found this form of denial through the limitation of memory difficult to comprehend. And then there was the eerie absence of memory in so many places. It was as if there had never been Jewish communities in places where once they had thrived. And then in little streets we would find the telltale signs of door-posts where *mezuzot* had once hung, or faded Yiddish writing faintly visible through subsequent layers of whitewash. Yes, whitewash. In many ways that's how I began to see so much of this, as a whitewashing of the past. Obviously there were those who hoped that a new fresh layer would cover over that part of the past which was best forgotten. As I stood in those forgotten places, I felt that at Beth Shalom we should clearly state that even though they are forgotten, we have not forgotten that they are.

I then spent several weeks in the United States. The Washington Museum was yet to open, but I zigzagged from Los Angeles, to Houston, to Detroit, to Florida, to New York and paid visits to no less than twelve institutions, all of which taught, documented, presented and archived the events of the Holocaust. There I found an enthusiasm and a sense of purpose, both at local and national levels, that I had not seen elsewhere. To list those institutions and their achievements is worthy of a book in its own right. What amazed me was how much more had obviously been achieved in the United States than in Europe, despite its physical distance from the events. What was troubling was the tendency toward an Americanisation of the Holocaust. Interpretation of events seemed to be tailored to meet the demands of an American audience who were sometimes only interested in what the Holocaust should mean to them as Americans, without a real understanding of its particularly complex European dimension. What I discovered was that in the vast majority of cases, these memorial institutions were either being created or funded by the Jewish community. This is natural of course, but it seemed to make them commemorative by nature, even when they supported important educational programmes. It strengthened my resolve to ensure that Beth Shalom should be different in that regard: while commemoration would be at the heart of the project, awakening a non-Jewish public from its apathy should always be the main objective.

At a different level, seeing so many institutions run and funded by the Jewish communities of the United States, I did have some niggling concerns about our identity as non-Jews dealing with the Holocaust. I was also continuing to find the personal discovery of the Jewish tradition very interesting and attractive to me. The more I learned about the Jewish faith, the more closely I identified with it. Historical learning over a number of years was now coming together with a personal encounter with the Jewish community on a daily basis. James and I found we were developing many, many new friends within the Jewish community in Britain and further afield. There were often times when we would find ourselves in synagogue or at commemorations or celebrations. Our smattering of Hebrew was always helpful when trying to get the prayer book the right way up and eventually follow the services more adeptly. What was initially an interest in the Jewish tradition developed into a persistent question: "Is this becoming not only an interest, but also a way of life? Surely, if we are so closely allied to the Jewish community, its past and its future, we would be better off as a part of that community and its future. Should we become a part of this destiny and convert to Judaism?" Actually, this interest had not developed from confronting the Holocaust, but from the previous years of encounter and learning, of which the Holocaust had become a significant part, bringing us even closer. James and I spent much time discussing this, in particular the theological implications of taking such a step. Is to convert to Judaism to desert the values of Christianity and deny the validity of the Christian message? If we do not feel theologically that we can convert, does it mean we are still allied to a supersessionist view of Judaism that will not allow us to 'go backwards', and hence remain part of the problem? If one abandons the supersessionism and respects Judaism for what it is, what is there to prevent one converting?

There were added complications in this issue in that my parents' training in theology and a life's work of commitment to the Christian church did not make it easy to broach the topic of conversion. We did spend a great deal of time talking about the Jewish tradition and the Holocaust, but actually to convert is a whole different thing, isn't it? I was aware that my parents knew their theological principles fairly thoroughly; while there was little doubt about their encouragement of our goals, changing identity in the midst of all of this might be another question. And then, just when I didn't think it was possible to admire my parents' insights more, Mother trumped me.

James and I were due to fly off to Berlin for a conference, and we had decided to meet from a variety of directions at Terminal One, Heathrow airport. My parents brought James to the airport, I flew in from the US and we met up as planned in the lounge. As we sat there having coffee, suddenly out of the blue Mother piped up and stated, "Your father and I have been talking, and although we think we would be too old to do such a thing, we imagine with all you have been learning that you might one day consider converting to Judaism. We certainly wouldn't influence you on such a matter, as long as you know that should you ever choose to do so, we would support you in any way we could." This came as an amazing surprise to me. Of course our parents knew about all our activities and interests, but we had clearly never dared talk about such matters as the theological implications of converting. While we lived in a home where faith was a key component of our lives, theology rarely was, at least not in terms of direct theological debate. However, I knew that for my mother to make that statement, having come from a conservative evangelical background, in addition to her own theological training, she had already weighed its consequences.

We did not convert, but it was not for theological reasons. In fact I would suggest that if any professing Christian is not comfortable theologically with the option of conversion to Judaism, then the question must be "Why?" It should not mean that all, or any Christians for that matter, should feel the compulsion to convert to Judaism, but at the same time, there should be no reasons why not. Put another way, if a Christian disdains the thought of conversion to Judaism, then clearly such an individual still holds the anti-Judaic seed of antisemitism responsible for a part of the context in which Nazism was able to grow. And that should not be. James and I had a number of reasons for not converting; firstly, because we became so wrapped up in what we were doing, we simply could not have found the time at that point. More importantly, we began to feel that part of the compulsion to convert was linked to our concern about the Holocaust, and we questioned the wisdom of that as a basis for conversion. You see, I once commented that it would be somewhat more acceptable to be dealing with the Holocaust if we were Jewish. Jim's reaction was as clear as it was definite: "If we were to convert, we would lose the potency of our message and conviction, and therefore have nothing more to say." To be from a Christian background and to deal with these issues is to confront the problem for what it is, and to encourage others to do likewise.

In this same regard we felt it was extremely important that the funding for the centre's initial development should come from non-Jewish sources. We did not make any large appeal, but went to the individuals and groups who had previously been sponsoring the centre and its development and asked them to extend their generosity to the new project. We also had learned, over many years, that project work could make good use of volunteer professional and general labour, saving substantial costs. In addition, by disposing of one or two assets belonging to the trust that were no longer in use, we were able to help fund some of the capital costs. In this way we were able to develop an important new project with relatively low costs and without having to approach members of the Jewish community with requests for initial funding. This we felt was important because certainly at its outset we had envisaged that Beth Shalom's contribution to understanding the Holocaust should be to stimulate non-Jews in general, and Christians in particular, to take an active participatory role.

CHAPTER EIGHT

VISION TO REALITY

There is a world of difference between planning something and making it actual, as we were about to discover. The Holocaust project was a vision and we were inspired to aim towards what we wanted to achieve. However, it is one thing saying that you want to create a memorial and exhibition, but where do you actually begin in practice? It is one thing saying you wish to take this to the British public, but what happens if they do not wish to hear?

There was a particular concern with this potential audience. We were creating a project in the middle of the Nottinghamshire countryside, at a time when public perception of the Holocaust was still very low. *Schindler's List* was yet to happen, as was the fiftieth anniversary of the liberation of the camps, both of which were to have a huge impact a couple of years later. We sat down with all of our plans and aspirations and asked ourselves what would happen if we did all of this and then nobody came or was interested. It was a telling question, not least because we had no reason to suspect that the British public would trek into North Nottinghamshire to confront a history they perhaps considered was now well in the past, and therefore of little significance to them. We decided that whether or not people chose to come, it was still important that we undertook the project, if only to say that there is something you can visit and learn from, rather than nothing. Then at that point should no one come, so be it; at least we would have tried. As it happens, I believe with hindsight that we were both right and wrong to draw those conclusions. Right, because if we hadn't taken the risk, Beth Shalom would not be contributing all that it does today. On the other hand, we were wrong to say that it was appropriate to have an institution just to say it was there. For any place to have meaning, it must be relevant to a constituency that subscribes to what it seeks to achieve. For that, one needs visitors who appreciate its presence. The visitors are its life, and without the visitors it has today, Beth Shalom would be no place, as it would make no contribution.

We decided upon a format that would allow a great degree of flexibility in terms of the spaces we had and their usage. We didn't want Beth Shalom to be a museum of the Holocaust: we didn't believe that any museum, however large, however well-resourced, however professional, could really do justice to either the scale of the Holocaust or the personal tragedy that it represents. Therefore, we felt that the exhibition space should be limited to a relatively small area of the total, so that discussion spaces, lecture rooms, libraries and learning facilities could provide our visitors with the opportunity to learn, to confront and discuss the Holocaust and its meaning for their lives.

With this in mind, we also knew how important the exhibition would be in focusing and reminding the visitor just what we are talking about when we enter into discourse about the Holocaust. We wanted to create a thought-provoking and meaningful exhibit that would not just repeat known historical facts, but place them in a suitable context. We decided that our exhibit should be about people and how they were affected by history. It should not only be about what happened, but to whom. We wanted to present something of the lives, the names and faces of some of the victims of the Holocaust. The balance between presenting the numbers, which in themselves are highly significant, and ensuring that individual suffering was not misrepresented, seemed hugely important. How could one convey, in the confines of a small exhibit, what this history meant to one individual, not to mention to countless hundreds of thousands of families right across the European continent? I had come to realise that the Holocaust was not about the mass murder of six million Jews, but about the suffering, the anguish, the fear, the pain, the murder of one Jew, and then another, and another, and another.

There was also a further issue. How does one convey to the average person with little concept of the Jewish tradition that Jews in Germany were not all the same, and that comparing communities in, for instance, Holland, Greece, Czechoslovakia and Lithuania, there was little in common at all? The vast cultural, linguistic and religious diversity that existed across the spectrum of European Jewish life mean that one cannot speak in this case of 'Jewish suffering' in the singular. Somehow we have come to use the term 'Holocaust' as if it were some kind of single experience that took place. This oversimplifies a very complex set of tragic events which affected and involved millions of people in very diverse circumstances over a long period of time. Clearly, the Holocaust was made up of tens of millions of experiences. And then to use categories of 'victims', 'perpetrators' and 'bystanders' undermines the complex nature of the way in which we identify individuals and their roles, and hence, what we can learn from them. To create pigeonholes limits the complexity of the experience and therefore restricts the lessons we can draw from it. Many victims were clearly only and always victims. But how far does the category of victimisation stretch? Was a non-Jew lying on a bunk beside a Jew at Birkenau any less a victim of those particular circumstances? And when he died in the night, was his death any less painful or significant than that of the Jew who died next to him? And what of the Jew who betrayed his fellow Jews? Was he a victim, a perpetrator or a different type of victim? And what of the perpetrators? Some were only and always perpetrators. But what of the Nazi who helped Jews to survive? Is he less of a perpetrator, less of a Nazi, or the type of perpetrator that many were – complex human beings? Does that make his perpetration of crimes against other victims less or more terrible? And what of the bystanders? Could there be such a thing? Surely if you stood on the sidelines and watched, you too were implicated through your passivity, allied to the actions of the perpetrators through inaction. What was worse: a sworn Nazi, who genuinely did not know that Jews were being taken to their deaths, who did nothing, or a cleric, dressed in the regalia of Christendom, who did know, and did nothing? And so one could go on and on. It was not so simple, and to make it appear so is to underestimate the serious issues that lie within it. Somehow we wanted to portray all of this in a meaningful way that would neither neglect the tragedy of the individual in the process of mass death, nor limit complex human history to simplistic analysis. We had to find a way.

We decided to create a 'memorial exhibition' within Beth Shalom that would not attempt to document everything, but to commemorate at the same time as explaining. It would be an educational tool to focus the visitor on what the centre is there to discuss, and why. In the exhibit we would begin by introducing the variety of Jewish life in Europe prior to the Nazi period and try to show the young and the old, the rich and poor, the religious and secular alike. We felt this was important as part of the context of the story we wanted to tell; after all, it was their story we were attempting to tell. One of the main frustrations we encountered was wanting to dedicate significantly more space than we had available to document and present more about the history, traditions and life of the communities that were destroyed. The question of who was destroyed seemed more significant to us than how it happened. We also wanted to avoid creating an impression, particularly for non-Jewish people who may be unfamiliar with Jewish history, customs and tradition, of the Jews as victims. All too often Jews have been the victims of western civilisation's penchant for persecuting its Jewish minority. But we felt that the life and soul, the struggle and dedication, the richness and poverty, that is, the diversity of the Jewish people, should be what captivates the imagination of an uninitiated audience, not its ultimate and seemingly inevitable victimisation. The problem of the victimisation of the Jews lay with the perpetrators, not with the victims.

Nor did we want to create a perpetrator-focused exhibition. It is easy to utilise the documents, photographs and footage of the Nazi propaganda units. It is comparatively easy to show how the framework of destruction grew and developed through Nazi eyes. It is easy to show the mass graves and the piles of corpses. But all of these, real as they are, were what the Nazis intended to create. This was their world, their version of history. They were not interested in the communities upon whom they inflicted their venom; they had already reduced them to a 'bacillus' in the body of the *Volk* that needed removing. As far as the perpetrators were concerned, the Jews were no longer human, so their version of history, their documents, photos and footage, their memoirs and excuses, while important, are not the whole history at all. They do not take into account the feelings, the hardship, the resistance and struggle for survival that Jews right across the European continent had to face, each day of their lives. Of course it is important to try to understand why the perpetrators did what they did. It is just as important to understand why so many chose the more convenient route of allowing the discrimination, degradation and destruction of the Jews to occur right under their noses in their own backyards. We must also recognise that while the handful able to muster the courage to care were clearly not enough, finding out why they did have such courage might give clues as to why others lacked this quality.

In the confines of the exhibition, we tried to draw out a few of these threads and highlight the complexity of the experiences. As well as outlining the context of Jewish experience, we also needed to explain the context of antisemitism and its long-drawn-out history in the western world, its origins within the Christian tradition, and its absorption into political, social and cultural structures, along with its development in Nazi ideology under the influence of the race sciences. This potent combination of precedents is such that until the mass murder of Jews following the invasion of the Soviet Union in June 1941, very little was unprecedented in Christian history in the centuries prior to the Holocaust. Forced separation, social and religious isolation, the wearing of distinctive yellow badges, forced ghettoisation, the burning of books and synagogues, restrictions on learning, professional practice and intermarriage, all these had been visited upon the Jews before. Only this time, it was more ferocious, more precise, more final.

The exhibition, we felt, should also give voice to the eyewitness. In this way, the creation of regular opportunities to read the words or hear the voices of those who were there, and to enter into their experiences, became important. If only through glimpses of their stories, we wanted to encourage our visitors to think about the real circumstances of real people caught up in the maelstrom of Nazi persecution. We wove into the text of the museum survivor narratives and diary extracts in which the experiences of individuals, including survivors who volunteer to speak at the centre, would be seen and heard within the context of the unfolding narrative of the Nazi era.

These include the reflections of Jewish diarist Chaim Kaplan, written at the moment of Germany's invasion of Poland. His almost prophetic words indicate just how much was known about the intentions of the Nazis:

> During the morning hours of the first of September, 1939, war broke out between Germany and Poland ... For the time being Poland alone will suffer all the hardships of war, because there are no common frontiers between Poland and her allies. We are witnessing the dawn of a new era in the history of the world.
>
> As for the Jews, their danger is seven times greater. Wherever Hitler's foot treads there is no hope for the Jewish people. Hitler, may his name be blotted out, threatened in one of his speeches that if war comes, the Jews of Europe will be exterminated...

The hour is fateful. If a new world arises, the sacrifices and the troubles and hardships will be worthwhile. Let us hope that Nazism will be destroyed completely, that it will fall and never rise again.

As Eastern Europe's new masters established ghettos for the Jews, the observations of the Mayor of Czernowitz provide an example of non-Jewish reaction to what they saw. Their perspective also seems important, if only to indicate just how much people really did know...

I looked out of the window of my bedroom and amidst flying flakes of early snow, I saw a scene which was incredible. In the streets a vast crowd of wandering people. The aged were helped by children, there were women with infants in their arms, cripples dragging their lame frames. All had bundles, their hands were pushing small carriages, loaded with boxes. Some carried their burdens on their backs: luggage, bundles of linen, cushions, blankets, clothing, rags. They were beginning their mute pilgrimage to their vale of tears, the ghetto. The majority of the working class Jews just wandered through the streets and alleys, pulling their pitiful barrows, carrying their miserable bundles and boxes until they sank exhausted in some corner or kerbside and could go no further.

And from within the blinding circumstances of mass death, somehow some individuals had the strength to try to tell us what they saw. Their reflections come right out of the camps and even the crematoria. Consider, for example, the words of the *Sonderkommando* who worked in the crematoria, entirely aware of the significance of the history in which they were involved. The *Sonderkommando* at Birkenau wrote in Yiddish or in special code, and buried what they wrote in the vicinity of the crematoria. Only after the war did the museum authorities overseeing Birkenau discover these notes, and among them, the words of Simon Lewenthal which we used in the memorial exhibition:

> The history of Auschwitz Birkenau as a labour camp in general, and in particular as the camp of extermination of millions of men will not remain – I am sure of it – sufficiently well handed down to the world. Part will be transmitted by civilians. But I think that the world knows a little about it even now. Surely for that reason we wrote it down...

Finally, we felt it important also to include throughout the exhibit a number of poems and reflections, some written by survivors and victims, some not. We wanted to stimulate visitors to think beyond the purely documentary and to have time, among the barrage of images and text, to stand back and reflect for a moment or two. Primo Levi and Dan Pagis are among the quoted authors, but perhaps most touching of all are the words of Franta Bass, one of the children of the Terezin Ghetto who wrote poems and drew pictures while in the ghetto:

The Garden

A little garden,
Fragrant and full of roses.
The path is narrow
And a little boy walks along it.

A little boy, a sweet boy,
Like that growing blossom.
When the blossom comes out to bloom,
The little boy will be no more.

One part of the centre I have thus far failed to mention is the garden. Beth Shalom sits in some three acres of Nottinghamshire countryside, on the edge of what is left of Sherwood Forest. Some say it is isolated, others that it is peaceful and quiet; either way, it is well removed from the clamour of urban existence. In this setting we thought it important to try to create an environment around the centre which would be both peaceful and meaningful; and so we created a garden. The garden is intended to be in counterpoint to the intense, stark images of the exhibition. In the quietness there is respect for the past, but also hope for the future. There are landscaped water gardens, with patios and areas for quiet contemplation. There is a memorial rose garden where hundreds of visitors have dedicated roses to the memory of loved ones lost in the Holocaust, or made general dedications of commemoration. A sculpture by Holocaust survivor Naomi Blake is at once personal and provocative. Entitled 'Abandoned,' the silhouette victim of Nazi persecution stands erect and dignified, asking the question, "Wherefore hidest thou thy face from me?", in protest at the abandonment of the Jews by God, yet full of the poise of a proud Jewish identity. Doreen Kern's 'Anne Frank' and Stan Bullard's 'Hidden Childhood' are pieces discreetly tucked into corners surrounded by foliage and garden aromas. Then there is the children's memorial, where thousands of visitors have placed stones in memory of the children murdered during the Holocaust. What I like so much about this memorial is that it grows and changes each day, and each day prayers, thoughts and wishes are added, some by Jews, some by Christians, Muslims, Hindus, agnostics or atheists. And every stone is there because someone wanted to remember by placing their own stone on the pile.

We realised early on in our planning of the centre that we should not even attempt to direct what visitors should think, feel or say. Instead, whether in the exhibition or libraries or out in the gardens, we wanted to provide the opportunity for visitors to draw their own conclusions, think their own thoughts, say their own prayers, that is, to enter into whatever discourse they felt was appropriate for them as individuals. In this way the garden is a good example of how survivors, teachers, students, clergy or lay people can be themselves without the imposition of competing voices and images, understanding themselves in relation to all they confront at the centre. It is a place of beauty, of memory and of hope.

CHAPTER NINE

IN THE PUBLIC
EYE

January 1995 was the fiftieth anniversary of the liberation of
Auschwitz and Birkenau by the Red Army. Somehow this had
come to be a significant event in the public's perception, and so I
decided I would go to Poland to experience what happened there
during the commemoration. I was not quite sure how to get close
to what was happening, and so I called the Polish press office, told
them I would be writing on the topic of the anniversary and
asked for a press pass. I was told there should be no problem, and
so I set off to Poland. That particular visit is another story in its
own right, but while I was in the lounge at Heathrow airport, I
received a call from the *Jewish Chronicle*. They had been told
about the forthcoming Beth Shalom project and wanted to cover
it that week in the Auschwitz Liberation edition of the paper.

On my return from a meaningful, and in many ways
revealing, commemoration at Auschwitz and Birkenau, there,
sure enough, was a picture of Beth Shalom on the front cover of
the *Jewish Chronicle* just below the story about the fiftieth
anniversary commemorations. It seemed somewhat strange to be
suddenly thrust into the spotlight on such an auspicious
occasion, not least because we had consciously avoided media
coverage of the project until this point. We hadn't wanted the
project to be 'hyped' in the press for the sake of a story because

the content and substance of the centre was, and always is, more important to us than media exposure.

Now the project took on a much more public dimension. The Jewish community was obviously curious about these developments and I was soon summoned to the Nottingham Jewish Representative Council to explain myself. The members listened patiently as I explained how the project had come about and what we hoped to do. At the end of my presentation, I wasn't sure what they would have to say about the imposition of Beth Shalom in the vicinity of their community. However, the chairman, David Lipman, went out of his way to welcome the Beth Shalom project and expressed immense pleasure on behalf of the council that it would be in the environs of the Nottingham Jewish community. To my surprise, I found the Jewish community across Britain equally warm in its welcome for the initiative. What came over, time and again, was a sense of satisfaction that Beth Shalom was confronting the Holocaust from a Christian perspective and was prepared to tackle the issues with clarity and honesty. Of course, I am sure that any Jewish person in their right mind, on hearing that an entirely non-Jewish foundation was starting a Holocaust project, would question the motives behind such an initiative. There was little or no reason to suspect that any Christian organisation would wish to take up the cause of confronting the Holocaust, and to do so honestly and with integrity, without at least some payback – which Christians seem able to achieve even when being repentant. And really, there is none of that intended. We are telling the story because it needs to be told, and told well to as many people as possible. These seemed difficult concepts to absorb, and so Beth Shalom needed careful and often personal explanation.

The general public was also somewhat circumspect. On one level people were prepared to accept, listen and take an interest in the Holocaust. *Schindler's List* had been screened by this time; the Holocaust was appearing on the school curriculum in England and Wales, and there was a growing awareness, particularly after the fiftieth anniversary of the liberation of the camps, that this was a real issue that still had not been fully dealt with. However, if there was to be a public expression of this, it might have been expected to come from Jewish sources in London or Manchester and not from a rural province. Local opinion was somewhat divided as to its merits in the area: some saw it as an imposition on an otherwise idyllic rural situation that did not need that kind of history. Others welcomed it as a fine asset to the area, that would focus minds on important issues. The regional press took it to be an important local project, with national and international significance. What was clear, however, was that people of conscience would waste little time in beginning to engage the issues it raised and would start to confront the Holocaust in a variety of ways in their schools, universities, churches and clubs.

For us, the dilemma was how to combine our professional lives with the project that was our real passion. James was a young medical doctor; I made my living manufacturing celebration cakes. We had both maintained our own professions as we felt it important not to earn our living from the Holocaust. Of course this made life complex: I had to leave my business unattended at times and James had to work long hours as a doctor, and then still contribute to the life and development of the project. At the same time we wanted to ensure that we didn't underestimate the necessity of being totally professional in our work on the Holocaust. We decided that we would work as a family team to run the centre. Mother would manage the day-to-day working and co-ordinate the administration. James would continue his career, but after a year or two would plan to take a couple of years out of his medical career to work full-time at the centre. I was to teach there virtually full-time, but leave some provision for maintaining my business. Somehow we have achieved a great deal with this combination of roles; because we were prepared to work for each other as well as with each other, I think our diverse lives have been rewarded, if at times they become a little pressurised.

We also had another concern as we entered the public eye. How would we ensure that Beth Shalom did not appear to be capitalising on developing public interest in the Holocaust? Obviously as a charitable foundation, no individual was to benefit, but we also wanted to ensure that Beth Shalom did not appear to be trivialising or commercialising the Holocaust. The easiest way to do that of course would be to develop it as an open-access public space, as larger numbers would mean more donations, more spent in the shop and hence more revenue. However, we felt we should avoid such a *modus operandi* at all costs: the focus should always and only be on education, discussion and dialogue. That said, the recent discussion around the so-called 'Holocaust Industry' has been annoying. The reality is that if you want to give your message, you have to be visible. To be visible you need to have the financial resources to support your work. To do that, you have to attract sponsorship, generate revenue and keep the organisation financially viable. There is no commercial gain in that. It is hard work to get a difficult message over. Amnesty International or Human Rights Watch are not berated for raising consciousness about Human Rights issues as some kind of 'Human Rights Industry' – it is understood that for their work to succeed they need public profile and financial stability. No less so in talking about the Holocaust. The alternative is not to do it at all, which is a different discussion altogether.

Prior to opening the centre itself, we launched an educational exhibit entitled 'Another Time, Another Place,' which was initially made available to schools. Very quickly we found that the exhibition was booked up months in advance, with some 250 young people each week benefiting from it. This interaction with schools before the opening of Beth Shalom created the foundation of important relationships with schools across the country, which would generate almost instant demand when we began our operation.

Finally, on 17 September 1995, the day came when we could say that Beth Shalom, our house of peace, was ready to challenge the British public with the need to remember the Holocaust, and to assume its responsibility to teach and warn future generations. In our minds, there was only one person who could possibly open it: our dear friend and mentor, the late Professor Geoffrey Wigoder, who had embodied so much of the Jewish-Christian dialogue since the Holocaust, but had also supported and encouraged us throughout our planning and creation of the centre. Our guests that day came from right across the spectrum of British society and among the audience were a great many survivors, for whom Beth Shalom became more than just an exhibition about a period of history in which they were involved. In many ways, it became their own place of memorial, their own Beth Shalom.

*Cutlery rusting in the open air at the
Kanada section of Auschwitz Birkenau,
1998.*

Above: Survivor Kitty Hart-Moxon signs copies of the revised edition of 'Return to Auschwitz', a part of the Witness Collection.

Left: Survivors Ibi and Waldemar Ginsburg with graduates from Lithuania on the Beth Shalom-Yad Vashem Summer School.

Left: A school pupil working in the memorial exhibition.

Below: James, a medical doctor by training, is also accomplished in multimedia, here working on the creation of a CD-ROM in the Beth Shalom design studio.

Left: Swedish Ambassador Mats Bergquist, accompanied by myself and survivor Gina Schwarzmann, opens the 'Gateway of the Righteous' on the occasion of the Centre's Sixth Anniversary.

Below: Receiving an MBE for services to Holocaust education, 2000.

Bottom: Discussing the exhibition with HRH The Duke of Kent on his visit to the Centre, July 2001.

Above: Survivor Arek Hersh, with members of a Beth Shalom party outside a church in Sieradz, Poland, where in 1942 he was parted from his family forever. He was told to join a work group, but his family was deported to Chelmno.

Above: Victoria Vincent tells her story to several young actors. Sadly she passed away three days later. Their memory of her story then became her legacy.

Left: Rabbi Emeritus, Lord Immanuel Jakobovits at the Children's Memorial, accompanied by his grandchildren.

Below: The Children's Memorial, where visitors can place a stone in remembrance of the 1,500,000 whose lives were so needlessly wasted.

Auschwitz survivor Trude Levi, lighting a candle at Beth Shalom's Yom Ha Shoah ceremony, 2002.

Top Right: Bergen Belsen survivor Rudi Oppenheimer lighting a candle at Beth Shalom's Yom Ha Shoah ceremony, 2002.

Top Left: Sam Pivnik, a survivor of Bendzin, Poland, stands by the images of 653 people from his home town, most of whom perished.

Below: Friends and colleagues from Lithuania, most of them non-Jewish scholars dealing with the Holocaust in education and the media.

Above: Mother, talking with young people from across the European continent. They are taking part in the Elkes Foundation's interfaith gardening week, organised by Sara Elkes, daughter of Kaunas Judenrat leader Elchanan Elkes.

Above: Addressing a group of visitors in the Hall.

Right: School pupils arriving at the Centre.

Below: 'Hidden Childhood', memorial donated by Simon Winston in memory of the Jews of Radzevilov who were brutally murdered by the Nazis in 1941-3. Sculpted by Stanley Bullard, 2001-2.

Above: Dr Nadja Smailligic, Bosnian refugee and participant in the Refuge Project, holding pictures of her family.

Jetmir Gjeta (right), Benjamin Ververa (below), and sisters Suzanna and Sijma Harustic (bottom), share their experiences at the Holocaust Centre with pupils from schools around Nottinghamshire engaged in the Refuge Project.

C H A P T E R   T E N

FROM PAST
TO FUTURE

There is a huge difference between the world that existed during the Nazi occupation of Europe and the one which young people inhabit today. It doesn't carry the same danger, the same uncertainty or the same concerns. Young men are not at war while their womenfolk work in the fields and factories; we do not need to carry ration cards or dig bunkers in our gardens. Ghettos and gas chambers and transports to the 'East' do not impose themselves upon this particular generation of Europeans. Most children live in a world which is safer, more sheltered and more protected, although sadly this is not the case for all, as we shall discuss later. Naturally, we crave that safety for them; we work for it, protect it and uphold it. But with that safety comes a certain complacency. Cocooned in the relatively safe environment of early twenty-first century western European life, how do you envisage something as removed as the Holocaust from your own personal experience? It is one thing talking about the ghetto and explaining its mechanisms; the starvation, the disease, the fear of death, the overcrowding, the will to live and the courage to resist. These can be described, but how do you really understand such circumstances? How does a teenager living in the relative comfort of suburban Britain relate to the utter deprivation and dehumanisation of life in the concentration camps?

We are faced with a serious problem in the future. How does one bridge the gap between what happened in the past and how we imagine it today? How do you teach a younger generation, detached from that past, and make it make sense not only within their world today, but perhaps more importantly, within their future? What can we do to ensure that our message does not trivialise the Holocaust, or turn it into a series of clichés that unintentionally belittle its complexity? These were some of the questions we found ourselves asking before the launch of the centre, knowing that many of our visitors would come with little or no prior understanding of the historical detail of the Holocaust.

One key question we had to answer was what kind of format we wanted to adopt in presenting the issues of the Holocaust to our respective audiences. We decided that initially Beth Shalom should not be a public gallery allowing an unsuspecting public to visit the 'World of Robin Hood' in the morning and 'do the Holocaust' in the afternoon. We wanted visits to be structured, educational and interactive. To fulfil this, most of our visits have been in essence educational seminars. Whatever the background of the group, whether it is from a school, a university or a church, the centre encourages them to engage with the topic, at their own level, rather than passively look on. Each visit is structured to attempt to open up new ways of exploring, researching, thinking about or discussing the Holocaust and its meaning for their own lives, careers or perspectives. Six years on, the decision was made to open to the public, too, in order to allow greater access to that broad group of people inadvertently excluded by our policy to focus on an in-depth quality experience.

The main focus of the centre remains with groups because we can give a deeper encounter, allowing more time with a focused group. And we achieve this by working as closely as we can with the group leader to ascertain something of the background and interest of the group. If they are a group of thirteen-year-old history pupils, their needs are likely to be different from those of a group of Sixth Form students studying moral philosophy, or a postgraduate museum studies group, a Jewish student union group, or group of senior clergy. The diversity of backgrounds necessitates a different starting point, a different set of focuses in discussion and different sets of goals and outcomes for the visit.

By way of example I will outline two different group types to show how varied the needs and interests can be:

Year Nine students (thirteen and fourteen-year-olds) who are studying history at school will tend to come in a relatively large group, who generally need to fulfil their curriculum requirement to learn about the Holocaust. The students themselves tend to be very diverse, with a wide range of abilities and cultural backgrounds. The vast majority will know very little. Prior to the visit we will work with the members of staff concerned to prepare the pupils as well as possible within the time constraints, encouraging teachers who have not visited the centre before to do so ahead of the school visit in order to better prepare the students. It is important that the students know where they are going and why, and what is expected of them.

The visit, which will last between three and five hours, is divided into three parts: historical exploration, understanding the personal tragedy, and analysis and discussion. On arrival at Beth Shalom, such a group will initially see a 20-minute introductory film about their visit and its aims. This is illustrated with archival images and covers the main historical points. It also demonstrates historical sources and encourages students to make full and appropriate use of them while investigating the Holocaust as history. They are also encouraged to think about the questions that the history of the Holocaust raises for them. The students then divide into smaller groups, one group in the exhibition, the other working with audio-visual presentations. If there are three groups, the third will work with photo workshops or art or poster exhibitions. The groups rotate until each has completed all the activities. At this age, students will usually work in the exhibition with an analysis-type worksheet to encourage them to consider carefully what they are seeing, and to begin the process of thinking it through. After a break, they will then spend an hour listening to a survivor relate his or her personal experiences and try to get a sense of how this broad history affected one person, one family, one community. This is a significant part of their visit for at this point they enter into the real lives of real people. Following that session, a survivor and one of the centre's professional staff members will, wherever possible, lead discussion with the group and try to develop a discourse around the issues that emerge from the experience. Very often questions are directed at the survivor, certainly on issues such as forgiveness or faith and beliefs (which incidentally are the two most common question areas for pupils of this age). The visit does not seek to draw conclusions from the Holocaust experience, but tries to raise the type of questions they are likely to need to continue to ask, for their immediate study and much further beyond.

Alternatively, a group of twelve ordinands who will shortly become parish priests and are attempting to get to grips with the Holocaust as part of their training, have a very different set of criteria to fulfil. As with the school group, we of course first consult with the group leader, or tutor in this case. On arrival, such a group will have a more question-based introduction usually conducted by myself or James, as we are more likely to be familiar with the type of questions they will need to address. The questions we pose centre around the causes of the Holocaust, including the long history of Christian antisemitism, the historical context in which it took place, and the kinds of issues it leaves in the contemporary world, in particular, in relation to the Christian environment. I will often also say something about the origins of Beth Shalom, how it came about and why, and through my own story and the challenges I encountered as a theology student, convey some of the challenges they may want to consider. It is also important that a group of this kind understands the global issues the Holocaust presents, particularly for

those in positions of moral and social influence. After an introduction the group will spend over an hour in the exhibition.
They will also usually hear a survivor speak, although for a
shorter time, as discussion forms an important part of their
encounter. After discussion with the survivor, we will spend time
in workshops reflecting on what has been encountered during the
visit and how that might impact upon their own learning and
future professional life. In particular we will investigate the
meaning of the Holocaust for Christian thought and practice,
including the persistence of Christian anti-Judaism, the Jewish-
Christian relationship and the challenge it might pose to their
future congregants.

The diversity of the two groups illustrates the need to be able
to address the same historical scenario from a variety of perspectives and at a variety of levels. Other groups that attend the
centre might cover as wide a spectrum as youth workers, race
equality officers, police officers, military personnel, victim
support groups, rotary clubs, etc. Clearly, in the personalised and
somewhat more intimate surroundings of a small, focused centre,
individual needs can be more readily met than in a museum
designed for hundreds of thousands of visitors. In this respect,
our goal is not only about raising awareness (although we hope
we do), but about challenging those who are aware, regarding just
how much – or how little – they have really questioned and
explored the meaning of the Holocaust for their own lives and
professions.

PART THREE
REFLECTIONS

C H A P T E R E L E V E N

LEGACIES

For fifty years we ignored them. Maybe we didn't know what to say. Maybe we didn't know how to say it. Perhaps we were just too busy building our own lives to care what had happened to others 'during the war'. Just after the end of World War Two, when victory was being paraded in the streets and relief swept over the long-embattled leaders of the world, among the debris of the conquered Third Reich were the remnants of the otherwise obliterated Jewish communities of Europe. The disease-ridden, starving band of survivors, who by a roulette combination of luck and design avoided otherwise inevitable death, had now emerged from the abandoned death camps. Their suffering, long ignored by the western world, suddenly became the focus of post-war propaganda efforts. Week after week the words "Now we know what we were fighting for...", broadcast to Saturday matinée cinema-goers, explained with perfect aplomb just how little they had really known what they were fighting for at the time. They certainly had not been fighting to liberate the camps or save the Jews, but of course no one was going to admit that once victory was secured. And the survivors sat in Displaced Persons camps, without families and without friends, without a past or a future. But now at last they were certain that the world would want to hear.

The Allies demonstrated their resolve to deal with this past by instigating war crimes trials for accused members of the Nazi hierarchy. Some were hanged, but the vast majority received relatively light sentences for their crimes. Once the trials were over, the public suitably informed and the process of judgement at Nuremberg concluded, the world could then refocus its attention on rebuilding the future and forgetting the past, not to mention facing the threat of its new Communist enemy in the east. And still the survivors sat in the DP camps waiting for someone, anyone, to give them a home. Those who did not go to Australia, Canada, the US or Britain began finding their way to Palestine, where of course once the State of Israel was founded, they thought everything would be alright. Actually, we now know that the Israelis were not very much better at listening to their brethren who arrived from the camps. They had a nation to build and they needed strong resolve to face the future of survival, not their past. And so the survivors had much to say, but no one to whom they could say it.

Today we have grown used to survivors in our midst. We film them, we tape them, we publish their memoirs and make films in their names. Day-in and day-out our media cover stories of long-lost relatives, restitution and the fight for a dignified end to what was an undignified beginning. Yet somehow we still struggle to understand exactly what they went through and what it should mean to us.

In the years running up to the opening of Beth Shalom, I had come to know a number of survivors around the UK, and had started to forge important working relationships with several individuals in particular. Kitty Hart-Moxon, Ben Helfgott, Trude Levi, Paul Oppenheimer, Abraham and Vera Schaufeld, Gina Schwarzmann and Victoria Vincent are among those who gave enormous encouragement to our efforts prior to opening, and there are too many to name subsequently. Our intention to document and include parts of their experience in the exhibition in turn led to discussions about the importance and place of survivor testimony in teaching about the Holocaust. I was aware that it remains a special privilege to be able to share with survivors: though they are in their latter years, they remain willing and able to tell their all-important stories to a generation for whom otherwise there is little with which to grasp such reality. Naturally, survivors cannot and do not tell the whole history of the Holocaust. Survivors tell their own particular experience as they have come to remember it. But from that comes an important dialogue across generations which can move, warn and highlight the consequences of prejudice and the road to mass death.

Survivors themselves are aware that nobody's memory is perfect and that every detail will not necessarily be retained or accurate. Survivor testimony is not a replacement for learning the history of the Holocaust, but it is a personal perspective which the historical facts alone cannot convey. The Holocaust is not only comprehended through its overwhelming enormity, but also through the enormity of its consequences for individuals. It is not only told through documents, but through voices, confusion, anguish and deep sorrow. At Beth Shalom, it is important to us that as many young visitors as possible, and most adult and professional groups too, have the opportunity to hear a survivor speak, not only to hear what happened, but also to talk about the consequences and meaning of the survivor's story for their own lives in the contemporary world.

Among all the stories of survivors who became involved with the work of Beth Shalom, that of Victoria Vincent is particularly moving. Victoria called me one day to see if she could come to the opening of the centre, and in the course of the conversation, I asked if there a particular reason why she wanted to come. She explained that she was a survivor of Birkenau and Auschwitz, and now lived in Nottingham. I went to see her soon after and found a lady in a wheelchair with a medical history that read like a medical student's textbook. We sat together as she told me her story. I realised from the way she shook as she talked that she had rarely told the story before. It was only later that I discovered I was virtually the first, after her husband and her doctor, to hear her tell her experiences. I suggested she should write her story down sometime and to my surprise she told me she had already done so, for the benefit of her grandchildren. Several weeks later we published her story, *Beyond Imagination*, as a memoir and educational text, and it became an important part of our library of resources. Over the next year, Victoria, who was otherwise virtually restricted to her home, travelled the country visiting schools and universities and spent many, many hours at Beth Shalom. When she died a year later, I found that I had lost a very dear and personal friend. I also discovered that the privilege of sharing with survivors today is one we must not underestimate. The conversations we shared together, and those that I have subsequently shared with many of my survivor friends and colleagues, remain some of the most important learning experiences of my life.

Soon their lessons will be legacies and we, the generations that follow, will have to carry the message they are trying to convey. That message is not just the experiences they endured, but what those experiences have come to mean. Out of the initial interaction between survivors and students, survivors and professionals, survivors and the media, survivors and the process of documentation, I soon began to realise that beyond testimony there is another layer of the relationship as yet not fully explored. In placing survivors in front of video cameras and asking them to say what happened to them, we create another document. Of course, that document will be invaluable to future generations and is therefore very significant. Those in the future who need to know what happened will be able to access wonderful, technologically sophisticated archives for that purpose. However, survivors have another story to tell: that is the story of how they have come to understand their own experience. Whenever a survivor tells his or her own story, he or she selects a number of episodes which have particular meaning. It might be about the loss of a loved one, or the day they realised that their fate was sealed, it might be about resistance or defiance, or justifying a certain act which may seem morally dubious in the 'normal world' outside the circumstances of the Holocaust; it might be about God, or human nature, or evil or good. Whatever the case, behind the text of the story are many perspectives which may not at first be apparent. In dialogue and discussion, these perspectives emerge and can develop into important and revealing conversation.

In bringing young people together with survivors, it is important that a conversation takes place beyond the telling of the story itself. In this way I hope that survivors of a generation who suffered the consequences of state-sponsored genocide can share, with the decision-makers of the next, what they understand by the experience and what may be learned from it. This is a fundamental principle, not least because the legacy that survivors leave is more than the narration of what happened to them: it helps us to make sense of all they endured and suffered.

The urgency to do this is clear. The passage of time will eventually take its toll and we will be left guessing about answers to questions we never thought to ask. Voicing those questions now and entering into discussion with survivors who are willing and able to contribute their reflections is, I believe, an important role for centres such as Beth Shalom to fulfil. They are witnesses, and one day we will have to convey their legacy. Through these dialogues, I think I share the hope of many survivors that in sixty years' time little boys will not have to stand in front of audiences as old men, weeping as they relay stories of the complete destruction of their families, friends and communities.

CHAPTER TWELVE

LANDSCAPES OF MEMORY

The Holocaust has not always been the prominent part of the cultural landscape it is today. In fact its development as an issue has been somewhat slow in coming. In some ways Beth Shalom has entered even that slow development late in the day, although remarkably it was the first such venture in Britain, and perhaps the first in the world to emerge from its particular perspective.

Initially, Yad Vashem, created in the early 1950s, emerged as the memorial that provided a necessary and important focus for survivors and Jewish communities the world over. Then it was perhaps the Eichmann trial in Jerusalem in 1961 that started the development of public discourse in the light of the Holocaust. This happened first in Israel, and was followed by a slow but steady stream of responses from a variety of places and disciplines. Survivors had tried, but now it was scholars in the late 1950s and early 1960s who were researching the period of the Holocaust. Through their study and publications they began creating the makings of a recognisable historical discourse on the Holocaust. Raul Hilberg, Israel Gutman, Karl Schleunes, Lucy Dawidowicz and Yehuda Bauer, to name but a few, produced seminal texts still read and re-read today. Then in 1978 Gerald Green's 'docu-drama' *Holocaust* was screened on American television and in other countries around the world. The film was roundly condemned by the survivor community as a fiction and a poor attempt to portray anything like the real situation, and with very good reason. However, from that point onward, Holocaust studies, representations, museums and education programmes began to grow with increasing rapidity. In the last twenty years we have seen a virtual explosion of writing, creating, building and dialogue around this difficult topic.

It did not happen all at once, of course; there were the milestones along the way. In 1978, President Jimmy Carter instituted the United States Holocaust Memorial Council which, fifteen years later, resulted in the United States Holocaust Memorial Museum. That same year, in November, Kitty Hart-Moxon took a British film crew to Birkenau and for perhaps the first time, a survivor described in some detail to an audience all around the world what had happened to her and hundreds of thousands of others like her. In 1985, Claude Lanzmann, who had been filming in Poland for some ten years, released his nine-hour, testimony-based film, *Sho'ah*.

From that point on there was little to stop the growth of interest. The fortieth anniversary of the liberation of the camps in 1985 was given time on television and radio, and public conscience began to grow. Films, books, memoirs, literature, analysis, history, theology, philosophy, oral history and audio-visual testimonies all started to emerge in greater and greater quantities. Conferences that previously had struggled to attract informed and interested audiences, were occupying larger and larger hotels and halls. When in 1988 Elisabeth Maxwell organised an international conference entitled 'Remembering for the Future', hundreds of scholars from around the globe converged on Oxford, and the field of Holocaust studies took another step toward general acceptance in the academic world.

Then the museums began to open. In America, the city of Detroit was the first to open a centre with an exhibition and education facility in 1978. Twenty years later, there are over one hundred members of the Association of Holocaust Organisations, most of them American, many with museum exhibits. Education institutes and bodies also began to develop rapidly. Organisations such as Facing History and Ourselves, the Anti-Defamation League, and latterly State legislatures in the USA have taken it upon themselves to ensure that students in particular are given opportunities to confront the Holocaust while they are young. Associated with this are important programmes in teacher training and graduate level studies, and, relatively recently, the first Masters programme in Holocaust Education at Richard Stockton College, New Jersey.

In Europe, of course, the situation was more complex because post-war the continent was divided. The Soviet Bloc sat like a huge immovable monolith on the doorstep of a confident but still confused West. Scattered right across the topography of the European continent were hundreds and thousands of camps and sites of mass destruction where the myriad victim groups of the Second World War had been murdered or worked to death. Holocaust memorialisation and education emerged as European governments decided what to do about these dark stains on their landscapes, and how to explain to young people how they came to be there. On the whole they preserved them, paid for their upkeep, and installed curators and museum designers to ensure that information was available for the curious public. However, the messages, particularly to the young, were very mixed. West German children learned history, history, history. Polish children learned that Auschwitz was the site of the martyrdom of Poland under the Nazis. The Soviets learned about the greatness of the Red Army in its heroic struggle to overthrow fascists who were murdering Soviet citizens. And the British learned virtually nothing.

Today, however, right across the world, there is an ever-widening community of people attempting to find ways of breaking down barriers between people and their memories, and building educational programmes which will bring people together to share in a common tragic past. Sceptics would argue that the process is driven by politics, commercialism, and the containment of memory. In part they would be right and great care is clearly needed to avoid such pitfalls. However, there are now serious centres and programmes dedicated to teaching about the Holocaust across America, throughout Europe, and as far afield as Australia, Argentina and Japan. Wherever there are people who really care about the values of humanity, people who share concern over our failures in the past and our direction for the future, there you will find someone who cares about the Holocaust and its impact on our conscience.

Following the demise of the Soviet Union, new opportunities exist in former Eastern Bloc countries, where archives have been opened and those responsible for tending sites of mass destruction are re-evaluating their message, not least because travel has become so much easier. As well as the institutional changes that are taking place, younger academics are beginning to address the topic of the Holocaust as their own concern, and its teaching is more widespread. Naturally, one has to be patient. It takes a long time for any nation to come to terms with its past, and for many of these countries the legacy of Communism is still a more pressing issue than the legacy of the Holocaust or the persistence of antisemitism.

However, through my own experiences I have come to encounter many courageous individuals working in the field of Holocaust studies who are presently making enormous strides. By way of example; in Lithuania, a country still struggling to assert its own post-Soviet identity and all too keen to minimise Lithuanian collaboration with the Nazis, it is easy to suggest that there is little hope for a serious programme of education and remembrance about the Holocaust. On the contrary. As in most situations, there are two sides to the story. While Lithuania has many internal and external controversies and the collective memory is predisposed toward antisemitic stereotypes and accusations, a growing group of historians, educationalists, sociologists and journalists is slowly forcing a confrontation within the society that will eventually impact upon what can be spoken of, where and how. Perhaps as a result of these strides and the serious engagement of the government there, Lithuania is able to take a leading role in working with other countries in the region, to help document, commemorate and teach that difficult part of this past. My own experiences in Lithuania of teaching teachers and working with interfaith groups and academics have been enriching and stimulating, with Lithuanians now incorporating their Jewish heritage more readily.

In South Africa, following a three-year development process (in which Beth Shalom was strongly involved from the outset), the Cape Town Holocaust Centre opened in August 1999. Whilst Beth Shalom was of course a non-Jewish initiative, the centre in Cape Town has been developed by the city's Jewish community. It is a valuable contribution to the 'New South Africa' where citizens are joining to seek ways to build a more tolerant post-apartheid society. In these developing environments, it is important that an external perspective is not projected onto a complex set of historical criteria, but that those who are willing and able to confront their own past and make their own bridges for the future should be given every support possible. The centre's success can be seen in the recent adoption of the Holocaust onto the national curriculum in South Africa.

Learning how to understand the sites of destruction and their meaning is not only an issue for the countries where the events happened and historical perspectives are still developing. It is important that those of us who are geographically removed also go to these places and sites too. In this regard, taking groups of individuals to places such as Germany, Poland or Lithuania is significant, not only to see what happened, where and to whom, but to understand further what and who was destroyed, what little is left, and to learn from the discourse in those places today. I am not talking about 'Holocaust tourism': visits which are either purely out of curiosity, or simply to look at sites for its own sake, or are so brief and superficial that they cannot be meaningful. I am talking about the kind of visit which allows time to confront and understand the world that once was, which probes more thoroughly the consequences of Nazi occupation. It should be sufficiently open to try and understand why others in the vicinity did not do more and why they find that history hard to face, and should give sufficient time to contemplate the awfulness of forgotten places like Chelmno, Belzec or Ponary. And if that were not enough, I also believe that visiting such places without meeting and talking with the people of those countries today is to place all of us in the path of danger once more. We have to learn to speak with one another at these places, to communicate and be honest about our fears and anguish; otherwise the hurt will never heal.

It is relatively easy to suggest that "Poles are antisemitic." On that basis, there is no good reason to deal with the hurt that exists around the Polish-Jewish relationship. It is more difficult to admit that while many Poles may continue to harbour antisemitic attitudes, some are also open to learning, and that a constructive dialogue can be engaged. If antisemitism is a problem in Poland, discourse, dialogue and education should be encouraged all the more. On the trips I frequently make to Poland, taking groups of students and teachers, we make a point of having a mixture of Jews and non-Jews to visit sites of former Jewish life, sites of mass destruction and to meet those in Poland today who are actively engaged in the social discourse. This, I believe, is where our future lies.

CHAPTER THIRTEEN

THE JEWISH-CHRISTIAN RELATIONSHIP

Cain and Abel provide the archetypal story of jealousy, competition and murder between brothers. The story goes that Cain slew Abel and then attempted to absolve himself of responsibility for the crime which he had committed. "Am I my brother's keeper?" he responds to God's enquiry about the whereabouts of his younger brother. Cain's answer was not to answer. Since the conclusion of the Second World War, amongst the many unanswered and perhaps unanswerable questions, one in particular challenges a reassessment of the state of relations between the Church and the Jews:

"Why does your brother's blood cry out to me from the ground?"

The problem facing Christians following the mass destruction of European Jewry is perhaps best understood as that of inadmission. Jews were murdered because they were Jews, and all of this in the context of a nominally Christian environment. Wholehearted opposition from the Christian churches to the so-called 'Jewish policies' did not happen, and so Christianity is in some way implicated, along with everyone else, in the crimes and their outcomes. However, merely to highlight the shortcomings of the Christian world might suggest that it had some moral high ground prior to the Holocaust. The crisis of credibility must only be a symptom of a more fundamental problem. Did Christianity lose credibility because of its failure to act, or was it fundamentally flawed in the first place? Further, and more troubling, was the Christian environment in some way causal, providing a basis or a context in part, on which the Nazis could build their anti-Jewish policies?

I began by explaining that an important factor in Beth Shalom's creation was a recognition of the need to address the Jewish-Christian relationship in its contemporary context. Now that the centre is functioning, and is used by Jews and Christians (and many others of course) on a daily basis, the question might be how the centre has contributed and is contributing to that relationship, or at least to what can be learned about it in light of the Holocaust.

The questions are disturbing if you are a practising Christian, not least because they are questions that must be asked. Further enquiry reveals that few Christians during the period itself demonstrated 'christian' behaviour. Conversely, many non-Christian people were entirely christian in what they were prepared to do. Ironically, the very religion that had lent its name to the virtues of moral humanitarianism was unable to demonstrate such qualities; and it certainly did not do so as an institution. Since the Church did not take the lead in instructing its Christians how to behave, the christian Christians who did take action did not demonstrate the credibility of their Christianity so much as their own humanity.

We understand the individual's demonstration of goodness by what she or he was prepared to do. It required saving someone, helping to hide someone or risking one's life to oppose injustice in some way. It meant doing something that was not required of anyone, but still needed to be done. In times of crisis, statements are generally considered sufficient for an institution to demonstrate a particular position and to indicate this to its membership. For the institutional Church to be effective, it had only to speak and its duty would have been fulfilled, at least in part. The silence of the Christian world clearly indicates the apathy and even treachery of its role.

Some ecclesiastical institutions made vocal, public and official stands against Nazi policy. The vast majority did not. The lack of understanding, leadership, or care in respect of the persecution of the Jews during this period amounts to negligence at best. Negligence implies that a clearly defined and understood responsibility was overlooked, with reckless disregard for the consequences. It also implies that the Christian Church cared neither about the Jews as people nor about what happened to them. Church negligence implicates it as an accessory to the outcome of the persecutors' actions; silence was complicity and participation.

The failure to understand the relationship between Judaism and Christianity – except in terms of longstanding enmity – ensured that Christian clergy were not equipped to evaluate their moral and fraternal responsibility, and furthermore often justified the persecution of the Jews as divine retribution. The Jews were the 'other' and that 'otherness' was sufficient to salve their conscience of any personal liability. If individuals can justify their (in)action through their ideology, clearly the theology behind it requires reassessment. How can people feel at liberty to behave in such a way and still feel able to call themselves Christians? In either case, the failure of professing Christians to act on behalf of the Jews demonstrates the abject failure of Christianity as a religion and Christian people as its representatives.

Among the many who did not act, the bravery of the few 'Righteous among the Nations' stands as a real example of human behaviour. The fact that many among them were practising Christians, including priests, pastors and bishops speaking out against the Nazis or assisting the Jews, illustrates the possibility of christian behaviour during the period. It is easy to hold them up as examples (and so we should). But at the same time this avoids addressing the question of their relatively small numbers. Why were these righteous people of Christian persuasion so often acting of their own volition? Their presence may demonstrate the possibility of christian goodness. That they were few in number may also demonstrate that it is only to be expected in relatively few cases.

The solutions to these desperately serious failures do not simply require Jews and Christians to be good to each other as they dialogue in a new-found friendship, however desirable that may be. Apologising and moving on will not address the fundamental fault-lines that have developed in the Christian tradition in a way which could form the basis of long term reconciliation. For Christians there are still difficult issues to face, which in light of the mass murder of European Jewry can no longer be ignored. In short, Christianity has to go back to its origins, its texts, its theology and dogma and take a thorough review. If it is not able to do this, its relationship with Judaism – and by extension with Jewish people – will at best be an uneasy truce.

For Jews, of course, the issues are entirely different. The presence or absence of God, and his ability to act or intervene, or his choice not to do so, are more likely to exercise minds or test the relationship between Jewish individuals and their faith. For the Jewish community, to struggle with identity is to struggle with faith in some respects. For some, to reassert the continuity of belief and therefore the acceptance of suffering as either divine or human, but nothing extraordinary, is the way to keep faith in spite of the Holocaust. For others, to protest to God or about God is the only way of keeping faith, whilst also letting their anguish or complaint be heard. In each of these situations, Jews are faced with issues concerning the continuity of the tradition, the maintenance of identity and the challenge of the future of the Jewish people.

In the Christian environment, the discourse has centred

around the antisemitic past of Christianity. Christians do not struggle with the nature, omnipotence, omnipresence or revelatory power of God in the context of their relationship with the Jews. Christians struggle with Christianity. In so doing they avoid the real disruption of the Holocaust. In fact, one may go further and suggest that much of the Jewish-Christian relationship engaged by Christians is about the defence of Christianity, rather than a challenge to it. The problem is, all Christians are Christian by conviction – Christianity is a choice. Jews are Jews, like it or not. To profess Christianity is to keep it, to justify it and defend it, because at the point you challenge it, you either cease to believe, or you believe something else.

Until Christians are prepared to face the possibility of losing Christianity in the light of the Holocaust, there can be no meaningful Jewish-Christian relationship. For this to exist, Christians must struggle with their own identity and memory, and be confronted with the possibility of nothingness. This sounds harsh, but in the light of the mass murder of European Jewry, not to face that potential loss is an insult to the lives of the victims. To date, I would suggest that there is no meaningful Jewish-Christian relationship because Christians have not yet put Christianity on the line as it should be. Dialogue does now exist, but dialogue can take place between any two individuals or groups. A relationship is something which is not formed in words (although words are important too), but in common understanding, shared experiences and aspirations.

As a contribution to repairing this broken relationship after the Holocaust, Beth Shalom is able to make inroads in highlighting serious issues for Christians. This is predicated partly on the fact that Beth Shalom as an institution sets an example to Christians that facing the implications of the Holocaust is possible for them. It also continues important work carried out throughout this century, in confronting the long history of antisemitism which is deeply embedded in the Christian tradition.

One of my great concerns about Jewish-Christian dialogue is the danger that it will merely be the stereo-effect of two entirely separate monologues. One side sits down with the other and politely tells one side of the story. The other expresses great interest and then proceeds to give the other side of the story in politically correct language, so as not to offend this new-found friend; and they each part company having talked to thoroughly nice Jewish or Christian people, respectively. The atmosphere is good; it is certainly better than avoiding or harming each another. To achieve a real relationship, however, one needs to be prepared to negotiate, to be open, to concede or change one's position in some way, and rarely does this actually happen.

It is in the face of this that Beth Shalom attempts to be a symbol of care, where care about the past has been all too absent; a gesture of good will after centuries of ill will; a sign of hope in a hopeless situation; a means of conversation when words have no meaning. Beth Shalom is not an admission of guilt, but a sign of responsibility. It is honest about the past and concerned about the future. And in that most troubled of relationships, Beth Shalom hopes more than anything to be a place of peace.

CHAPTER FOURTEEN

THE HOLOCAUST
AND THE FUTURE
OF WESTERN
CIVILISATION

The questions remain unanswered, "How should the Holocaust impact upon our lives in the contemporary world? Are we studying, investigating, uncovering this because of the past, or because of an underlying concern about the future?"

The destruction of European Jewry as an historical event within the context of western civilisation is reason enough to spend time, energy and resources to better understand what happened and represent it to a wider community of people. Whether or not there are lessons to be applied from that history, it is important for any individual who is so moved to contribute to a meaningful commemoration of the Jews of Europe. Their lives and talent were wasted, their contribution or simply their presence within the communities of Europe was a sufficient loss for us all to feel the effects and mourn them as our own.

But behind the events themselves lay a number of causes. These unseen or often unaccounted-for causes are the real concern, because without them, men, women and children would not have been gassed and burned. Clearly, without the ambitious leadership of Hitler or the pernicious race ideology which singled the Jews out for destruction, none of this could have happened. But it took much, much more than that. There were literally thousands of agents who instigated, orchestrated or carried out the murders. There were millions of individuals, active or passive, who helped the process along or who did nothing. Of greatest concern in all of this, is that despite claims that the Germans were predisposed to doing such things, the vast majority of Germans who were involved made the kind of choices that anybody might make in the same situation. Over a period of time, they were able to carry out barbarous crimes against humanity and feel no sense of shame or guilt; on the contrary, they saw themselves as contributors to the great Aryan good.

Underlying this is a concern that anyone can create a dream civilisation: the utopia to solve all the ills of the world. Then, provided there are sufficient beneficiaries from what that civilisation has to offer, the losers, the persecuted or the destroyed will not matter. The ethical considerations raised by this are very clear. Historically, the victim's experience of genocide is always different. What is disturbing is that the mechanisms of perpetration and the reaction of the bystanders in such crises are generally quite similar.

One of the questions we asked ourselves in setting up the centre is how we could contribute to a better understanding of the path to genocide. It seemed important to alert our visitors to the fact that although they might feel that everything in their own lives was going smoothly, the path to genocide begins in unsuspected places and every act of intolerance and discrimination must be taken with the utmost seriousness.

A fundamental question to ask in respect of personal responsibility and ethnic persecution is, "When does one start to intervene?" When the gas chambers are burning and the trains are arriving daily? When the ghettos are full and their inhabitants starving to death? When war begins and villages are torched and synagogues burned? When political leaders threaten mass murder? When, and if, war begins? When persecution drives people from their work and children from their schools? When laws dictate who can and who cannot be citizens? When parties include the threat of ideological persecution in their election manifestos and make the scapegoats of a faltering society a matter of public concern? Or is it when somewhere, at some time, you hear a remark about 'them,' those people considered outsiders who might just become the scapegoats in the manifesto, who may no longer be citizens of their own country and are driven from their jobs and schools, who are threatened with death, whose villages are torched and synagogues burned, who are starved in the ghetto and daily put onto trains and burned?

When we can answer this, I believe we will be better placed to say we have understood the Holocaust. It does not undermine the immense tragedy we are trying to commemorate, nor detract from the singular importance of understanding the enormously complex issues that surround the Holocaust as an historical experience. It simply reinforces the understanding that at the time of the Holocaust there were simply too few individuals who understood enough, or did enough, early enough. So often we say that we did not know about what was happening in Europe during the Nazi occupation. But in actual fact, the events of April 1933 should have been enough. The question is whether or not they would be even today.

In our quest to understand, we should be careful not to oversimplify things. When I try to comprehend the Holocaust, I know that I struggle to get to grips with it for a whole variety of reasons. Historically, I know that it is an event I will never really understand. A set of events that took place over twelve years, in over twenty countries, involving literally millions of people, is a set of events I know is beyond me. I could spend my life trying to understand the complexities of Weimar Germany and its transition to the Third Reich, and the metamorphosis of the German people with it. I could spend my life studying occupied Poland, or France or Greece. And having completed my research on a chosen topic, I might well draw my conclusions, only to admit that after a lifetime of research, a great deal was still left unclear.

Similarly, I know that I will never understand the personal tragedy of the Holocaust. I spend much time with survivors, listening to their heart-wrenching stories and trying to comprehend the pain of survival and all they have had to live with. When writing the foreword to the book of my good friend Waldemar Ginsburg, I found myself with a real dilemma. Here is a man who sat with thirteen members of his family in Kaunas, Lithuania in June 1941, deciding whether to flee to the Soviets or stay under the occupation of the Nazis. Older members of the family had experienced German occupation in the First World War and could vouch that the Germans were civil enough then. Younger members of the family had just returned somewhat disillusioned from the Soviet Union, and so they decided to stay in Lithuania. A few years later, he was the only one of that family group still alive. So, as I sat down to write, I had to ask myself what right did I have to write the foreword to a book containing experiences I clearly cannot understand? What do I know of starvation and thirst, incarceration in the ghetto, working in the winter cold with little protection, mass shooting and selections and the struggle for survival, day after interminable day? And what do I know of having twelve members of my family shot, beaten, dragged away in front of my eyes, or pushed overboard at sea? What right do I have to write about such things?

I found that I had no right to do that.

But I also found that I do have a responsibility, if only to try and explain how little I comprehend such things; how much I struggle to conceive, let alone relay, issues relating to the Holocaust.

There is something, however, that I feel I do know, and it pertains to the topic of this chapter. I do know that the Jews, as the victims of National Socialism's campaign of discrimination, isolation, deportation and mass death, were not looking for other

Responding to the Kosovo crisis, April 1999: planning the appeal (right), sorting the mountains of aid donated by the public (below), and delivering the aid to refugee camps on the Kosovo-Albania border (bottom right). With media, public and business support, within eight days the East Midlands Kosovo Appeal was able to despatch 15 lorryloads of aid.

Below: Film-making is an increasing part of the Centre's work.

Above: Retracing with Kitty Hart the route of her death march across Poland for the BBC documentary 'Death March: A Survivor's Story'.

A range of resources, literature and films produced at the Centre.

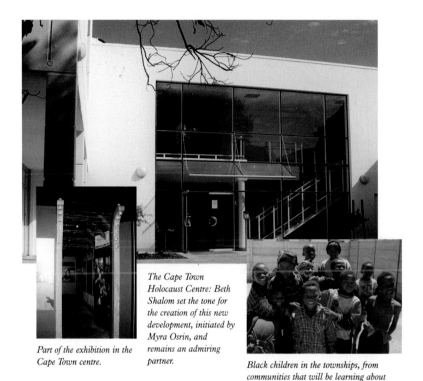

Part of the exhibition in the Cape Town centre.

The Cape Town Holocaust Centre: Beth Shalom set the tone for the creation of this new development, initiated by Myra Osrin, and remains an admiring partner.

Black children in the townships, from communities that will be learning about the Holocaust through visits by their schools to the centre.

Anna-Karin Johansson and I discuss the 'Living History' project, initiated by Swedish Prime Minister Göran Persson in 1997.

Images from the inaugural national Holocaust Memorial Day. Inset: Survivor Anita Lasker Wallfisch talks with liberators of Aushwitz and Bergen Belsen, General Vasily Petrenko (left) and Major Dick Williams, during the HMD ceremony at Beth Shalom, January 2001.

Top: Lilian Umutoni, the City Authority's manager for the project, discusses Kigali's future genocide memorial centre in the empty buildings at Gisozi (left) with Jim. 250,000 victims of the genocide are buried in close proximity.

Below: Claire Kabahizi at Nyanza, Rwanda 2002. Her parents and other relatives were among several thousand Tutsis slaughtered there by Hutu militia in 1994.

Rwanda 2002: Surrounded by children while filming (top); genocide survivor at Bisesero (left); bones and clothing of victims still lying in the Ntarama Church where they were murdered in 1994.

140

Top: Foreign Office Minister Peter Hain presents General Romeo Dallaire with the inaugural Aegis Award, January 2002.

Right: Aegis executive members, Richard Rubenstein, Carol Rittner and Hubert Locke with Linda Melvern, author of 'A People Betrayed: The role of the West in Rwanda's genocide'.

Bottom: Delegates take part in the landmark Aegis-FCO Genocide Prevention Conference, January 2002.

Jews to come to their assistance at that time. In any given situation of persecution or mass death, the victims are never best placed to act as advocates on their own behalf. In a genocidal situation, agents are needed outside the victimised group who are prepared to act or intervene on their behalf. Naturally, if the Jews of Britain, America and the Yishuv in Palestine could have done a little more, or been more alert and aware and prepared to speak out, then that would have been for the better. It is an important discussion to have, and the Jews of the free world of the time need to examine their conduct closely. However, the Nazi party was not likely to listen to a group of Jews in New York telling them how to run their racial state. What was required was the conscience of the world, of governments, of academia, the media and all those who cared about the fate of others to speak out and make an impact upon the situation. That doesn't mean to say that they would have been successful, or that the outcome would have been any different. At least we could have said that we tried, that humanity had its day and that no stone was left unturned in a bid to do whatever was possible.

Sadly, those voices were not there; the Jews were not a priority for the governments of the day. Blame for the decline toward total destruction cannot be levelled at anyone except those who carried it out. Responsibility for the unhindered manner in which that genocide took place lies fairly and squarely at the door of the powers of the time, and should be taken as such.

All of these rather sweeping conclusions are fairly easy for me to reach, as I am a generation removed from the events and have the benefit of hindsight. However, I personally am not best placed to make judgements on such matters. Firstly, I was not there and do not know how I would have reacted. I would like to think that I would have been the one who wrote the all-important letter that would change public opinion and rally the masses to the aid of the Jews. I would like to think I might have been the politician in power who would make the vital speech and change government policy towards a more humanitarian outcome. In reality, I suspect that like the vast majority I would not have known what to do, or would simply have chosen to do nothing. Secondly, in my adult lifetime there have been a number of genocides or genocidal situations of note, one in Bosnia Herzegovina, the other in Rwanda (and many others if you care to count). In terms of their historical significance, one might argue that they were not on the same scale, or were not as long and drawn-out, nor were the long-term ramifications as serious as for the Jewish communities of Europe whose whole civilisation was all but wiped out. Of course they were not the same type of genocide as the Holocaust because no two genocidal situations are the same. What concerns me is what I did about them. Because I didn't do anything of substance. I wrote a few letters and made a few calls as people were dying – no, being murdered – in my backyard.

If 'evil triumphs when good men [and women] do nothing,' then if I consider myself 'good' in any way, some kind of action is required of me when I see something evil happening. If this is another 'lesson of the Holocaust', it is a demanding one: it requires you to act on behalf of somebody else, which seems contrary to human instinct. And then, what of the few brave souls who did do something and in spite of their actions, evil is still seen to have triumphed? Was their goodness less good than the evil or were there insufficient good people to outweigh the evilness of the evil people? Or did the few evil people have more who were willing to follow their example than the good had to follow theirs? If one thing we learn from the Holocaust is that we are required to act, another is that we might not be successful in our efforts. That does not mean we should not take action, otherwise the Righteous among the Nations were wasting their time and no one will ever do anything like that again.

I am struck by the human message that this contains. While the Holocaust itself might have been unprecedented in human history, the motivating forces of racial discrimination and ethnic hatred are a tragically universal phenomenon in which the potential to repeat mass death may lie in wait for future unsus-pecting victims. At the same time, the goodness and the will to resist that demonstrated itself, must also be a universal principle that can be motivated for the common good. The question we must ask, as educators and facilitators of our history, is how to encourage the principles which contribute to the creation of a more peaceful world in which to live.

This is something I feel I am beginning to learn. As we approached the Easter Bank Holiday 1999, hundreds of Kosovar Albanians were being massacred and tens of thousands forced out of their homes and their country by Serb forces, against whom NATO was waging an air war. James and I realised that as directors of an institution claiming to address the issues raised by the Holocaust, we could not ignore the situation. We initiated the East Midlands Kosovo Appeal, both as an expression of our concern and as a means of concrete practical action. Perhaps a little to our surprise, this sparked such an overwhelming public reaction that within several weeks, we were able to deliver hundreds of tons of aid for the refugees camped in Albania and Macedonia.

The necessity to identify and warn of the potential for genocide is something that all those dealing with the Holocaust should be prepared to do. It seems to me that our goal in Holocaust education is not to prevent genocide against Jews as a consequence of antisemitism (although that is obviously part of it). Rather, it is to prevent the waste of human life, anywhere, at any time.

People suffer all over the world all the time. Each person's suffering is different because suffering can never be compared. To compare the suffering of those who are murdered in acts of injustice is to insult the victims and all who share their fate. This is not about who suffered more or less than anyone else because what one individual suffers in any given situation, another feels equally in another time and place. Beth Shalom documents the suffering of the Jews under the Nazis, not because Jews suffered more, but because Jews suffered. In this world of troubling and oft-repeated persecution, we do not need comparison, we need compassion. It is part of the goal of Beth Shalom to see how that compassion can be found because certainly, and sadly, it will be required of all of us again in the future.

CHAPTER FIFTEEN
WHAT NEXT?

As a result of the East Midlands Kosovo Appeal, James and I travelled out to Kosovo, Albania, and to Macedonia in different capacities. James went out to be a volunteer physician for the International Medical Corps. Based in Kukes, Albania, he and his colleagues were involved in helping with the refugees who had flooded into the town and in repatriating the Kosovar Albanians after the conflict came to an end. I found myself on several occasions down at the Stankovec refugee camps outside Skopje, Macedonia, attempting to understand the immensely complex aid need and network.

Standing on the border watching the line of refugees snaking back into the Kosovo hills from the Macedonian checkpoint, it was clear to me that we were witnessing a lucky escape; that is, if the stories were true that most Albanians had survived. It was not the sort of terrain you send a small group of soldiers into to take the country. It is beautiful, rolling countryside, which in places is quite mountainous. There was virtually nowhere for advancing troops to hide and plenty of vantage points for defending forces. Mr. Blair and Mr. Clinton seemed quite proud of their stout-hearted defence of the Kosovar Albanians. There was good reason to be proud on one level, as their efforts – particularly those of Mr. Blair – compared very favourably with many countries that did not assist in the conflict at all. But it was also clear to even the most ignorant military strategist, that if Mr

Milosevic's 'final solution' (as his policy was described), was anything other than pushing the Albanians over the border, then there would have been one more genocide in the twentieth century that left us standing. Fortunately for the victims, that was not his intent. Or if it was, it was never implemented. The brutality of their eviction, the organisation of his troops and the determination of his policy should have rung the loudest alarm bells that Whitehall has available. There was a reaction eventually, but not before hundreds of thousands of people were displaced. Thankfully, the majority were ultimately able to make their way home, however tragic the homecoming was in many cases.

Genocide did not occur in Kosovo. But preventative policy failed again. The only reason that the Kosovar Albanians are still alive, is because Mr. Milosevic did not kill them; not because we saved them. This time James and I understood this more intimately, because we were seeing it with our own eyes and hearing it with our own ears.

This experience was to influence our thinking deeply. We decided that we needed to create a vehicle for predicting the development of genocide, and to mitigate its effects much earlier than the ineffectual scramble in Kosovo. We knew that we had let those people down, even though they didn't seem to realise it as they waved their 'Thanks NATO!' flags. Before the outbreak of the crisis, we had been planning the extension of our work through the creation of Aegis, a new organisation we envisaged would work alongside the Beth Shalom Centre and assist the implementation of the 'lessons of the Holocaust' in practice. We envisioned that Aegis (which means 'protection'), should address the fundamental issues within society that allow the fault-lines to appear, which then facilitate the onset of the environment in which genocidal ideas can grow and succeed. Then, as we looked at the crisis in Kosovo, we decided that we should press ahead with the Aegis project in order to focus on strategies for the prevention of genocide.

WHAT NEXT?

Aegis came formally into being in 2000 with the aim of bringing together a wide spectrum of scholars, journalists, non-governmental organisations, governmental departments and international organisations in order to assess how such a cross-sector group could best facilitate the implementation of preventative strategies. We were aware from the outset that this was a task too large for any one organisation, but one that needed to be shared across a wide and talented group. We found ourselves supported by respected scholars of the Holocaust with serious intentions in supporting our goals. John Roth from Claremont McKenna College, California, Hubert Locke from Washington State University, Carol Rittner, from Richard Stockton College, New Jersey, Elisabeth Maxwell, founder of 'Remembering for the Future' and Richard L. Rubenstein of the University of Bridgeport, Connecticut, were the members of our initial executive. These scholars alone had over a hundred and twenty years of teaching and researching about the Holocaust between them collectively! Along with that, they also had a real desire to see its implications taken seriously in the prevention of future genocide, and the impact of their work was significant. From this initial group of trusted friends, the development of a serious and committed network of prevention specialists has come into being which provides a platform for changing the environment for preventative policy.

In January 2002, Aegis held what amounted to the first cross-sector conference on the prevention of genocide in which academics, government departments, military personnel, journalists and non-governmental organisations discussed the real possibilities of moving strategies forward in a meaningful way. The gathering was a joint project with the UK Foreign Office, who saw the need to engage the debate as a policy issue. Working on behalf of Ministers, Alan Weeks and James Roscoe of the War Crimes Section showed the kind of vision necessary in Foreign Policy-making to create important links between past events and future preventative policy. Convening such a conference, which may evoke criticism, is as courageous as it is necessary. It becomes ever more clear, however, that making these changes is going to be hard work, because political will is associated to perceived national interest, and if neither the interest of the electorate nor the economic interest of the country is at stake, then providing resources to prevent the build-up of genocidal ideology is going to be difficult to achieve. And this is the real point. It takes both political will and financial resources to make primary (early) prevention possible. If we do not act early, then we begin to gamble with people's lives as we did in Bosnia, Rwanda and Kosovo; and as we have learned, when you gamble, sometimes you win and sometimes you lose. And when you lose, the results are catastrophic.

Reducing the risk means being committed to the cause of humanity and being somewhat altruistic in our foreign policy. As an electorate, being clear about the demands we place upon our politicians is the first step. One of the biggest dangers of democracy is that it can be self-serving. That is, the first priority of the voter – myself included – is by and large to choose a party that most suits my own personal needs and interests. Therefore, politicians address those needs as they perceive them to be – or as the focus groups tell them. Health, education, economic stability; these are usually the issues and of course they are important attributes of any nation's well-being. But how many people actually vote – or not – based on their expectations of a given party's human rights agenda? How many parties would even think to include their conflict prevention or international aid policy in the manifesto that drops onto your doormat?

Aegis was not long in existence before it realised that in order to make changes to the way governments behave, it is also important to inform the public. And so Aegis soon became more closely associated with the day-to-day work of Beth Shalom in attempting to highlight the need to understand the path to genocide with the visitors to the centre. We had initially attempted to keep the two organisations distinct from each other, but there is a natural magnetism. Actually, in teaching about the Holocaust, we introduce a moral imperative to be active in defending the rights of the vulnerable, identifying ideological hatred and violence and rooting it out, wherever it might be. In this regard Aegis is the perfect and natural partner for Beth Shalom. It needs to take its message and apply it in a number of educational and practical environs.

The partnership between Aegis and Beth Shalom has resulted in a significant increase in the output of the organisations. Aegis Productions and Aegis Publications are now both functioning units at the centre that produce educational materials, documentary films, academic publications and internet-based resources. The concept is to make an effective communications team that can produce high-quality, challenging materials that will reach wider audiences. With the advent of the internet and the ever-shrinking global environment, it became clear to us that we need to have the tools to reach a very far-flung range of people, because our message is just as pertinent in Asia as it is South America, as it is here in the UK. Genocide is a global issue. Therefore we need to develop global reach with our message.

Over the next three years, we aim to develop a permanent Aegis Centre adjacent to Beth Shalom. If plans succeed, it will contain the world's first museum on the history of genocide, which will detail thematically the ways in which genocide emerges and the consequences of its implementation. There will also be a research and policy centre which will work as a think-tank on preventative policy. The Aegis Centre will be situated on the same campus as Beth Shalom and will share many facilities.

Developing this concept, however, raises new philosophical questions. There is no doubt that anyone involved in teaching about the Holocaust wants to make a difference to the world in which we live. That is presumably why we do what we do. How to balance the need to explain the specific experience of the Holocaust, with the equally important need to find practical applications across a range of circumstances that raise similar issues, is a more complex undertaking.

In the world of Holocaust education and scholarship (as well as for survivors and their families), there are many fears that genocide issues might more generally relativise and dilute the message of the Holocaust. Those fears are well-founded in some respects, as there are many people, particularly on the left of the political spectrum, who would prefer to include the Holocaust in the general area of human rights. This way they can inappropriately equivocate the Holocaust with a range of issues, and avoid its real challenge. This relativisation cannot be justified on a whole range of levels. The Holocaust was unprecedented and horrifying in its scale and implementation. That said, those who really understand the Holocaust for what it is, have a duty to take its message to inform the environment in which we live. We should be more prepared, more able to confront hatred and to fight for the human rights of those who are oppressed, and to seek to help heal the pain of the survivors of more recent atrocities, ethnic cleansing, and genocide.

Over the last few years, there has been a growing awareness of the need to incorporate the challenge of genocide more broadly into the research that is being conducted into the Holocaust and its consequences. Increasingly, departments and centres which teach about the Holocaust have included 'Holocaust and Genocide' in their titles. By way of example, the recent Remembering for the Future 2000 international conference, the brainchild of Elisabeth Maxwell, had 'The Holocaust in an Age of Genocide' as its subtitle. It brought together in one forum both Holocaust and genocide scholars, who successfully contributed over two hundred papers on facing the challenge of the Holocaust in an age in which genocide persists.

The vision behind Remembering for the Future is an important one, which is also to have an impact on the future of Beth Shalom. Elisabeth Maxwell and her colleagues ran the first RFTF conference in Oxford in 1988, with the sponsorship of her late husband. Elisabeth is a scholar of substance in her own right, with an important interest in the Jewish-Christian relationship after the Holocaust. When she established the conference, Holocaust studies was still only in its infancy, with new disciplines beginning to realise the relevance of the Holocaust to their various fields of interest with increasing momentum. The Oxford conference was a significant rallying cry to scholars to continue to develop their focus and engage the issues in an inter-disciplinary manner. Subsequently, two more RFTF conferences have occurred, one in Berlin in 1994, the other in Oxford again in 2000. Elisabeth Maxwell has now retired from the hard work of organising conferences, and has entrusted the future of RFTF to Beth Shalom. The intention is to have an annual cycle of academic lectures, symposia and publications around a given topic each year, thus changing the emphasis from intermittent large conferences to small regular symposia. Hopefully, this will allow the five hundred scholars associated with RFTF to be able to find a continued outlet and networking from their engagement on a regular basis. It is also envisaged that the circle of both Holocaust and genocide scholars from a range of disciplines will address the difficult issues raised by this academic research.

Scholarly work of this kind is important, but the grass roots connection to the people who are most affected by the conse-quences of genocide must always be our priority. After all, it is their lives we are talking about. Recently, James has been working with survivors of the genocide in Rwanda to see if there are ways in which Aegis can help tell the story of that genocide and assist in drawing the necessary conclusions from it. He has spoken to many survivors of the genocide, who have been left without their families, without their children, without a home, or employment, or who may be dying from HIV/AIDS as a result of the gang rapes during the genocide. Time and again, he has expressed his anger and frustration that once more, a vulnerable group of people who need to be heard and understood are left to suffer in silence. Seven years on, many of the survivors have yet to bury their dead. Some even refuse to bury them "because the world will forget what happened to us..." They know we have short memories.

The genocide in Rwanda was one of the travesties of the twentieth century. It was a double-edged sword too, a dangerous conspiracy of outright evil and wilful inaction. This was not an event enacted a generation before my birth. This time I was a twenty-seven-year-old voting member of the British public, who, like many, sat in front of the television and watched it all unfold in front of my very eyes... and still did nothing. The perpetrators were clearly the Hutu Power regime and its organised network of militia, who slaughtered the best part of a million people in twelve weeks. But it was not possible without the connivance of the UN, which withdrew its activities in the country after the killing began. Reinforcements would have prevented the genocide, as General Romeo Dallaire, the very capable leader of peace-keeping operations, made clear to his colleagues in New York. But around the Security Council table, there was no intention to risk the lives of UN soldiers. And so women and children died instead – and in infinitely larger numbers. In January 2002, Aegis inaugurated its international award "For Altruism, Resourcefulness and Bravery in Preserving the Value of Human Life", which was presented to Romeo Dallaire. Although his mission failed to prevent or end the genocide, it was not without a tremendously courageous effort on his part, and thousands of Tutsi – the ethnic group targeted for killing – do owe their lives to his efforts and those of others like him. In presenting the award to Dallaire, Foreign Office Minister Peter Hain stated: "General Dallaire, as commander of the UN Assistance Mission, found his warnings of impending calamity discounted and disregarded by his superiors in the governments – including that, I am sorry to say, of the United Kingdom – to which they were reported. The tragic consequences have left a stain on the collective conscience of the World. We failed to prevent genocide." That the Foreign and Commonwealth Office recognises this need for change should give us all a degree of hope in the face of future conflicts. However, the resolve will only be known when it is put to the test.

In the meantime there is still much to learn from the recent past. Aegis has recently embarked upon a project to build a centre similar to Beth Shalom in Rwanda. Unlike Beth Shalom, it will be built adjacent to one of the killing sites at Ntarama in the Nyamata district, about an hour's drive away from Kigali. Like Beth Shalom, it will have a memorial aspect, with gardens and reflective spaces. It will be a place of learning with an exhibition about the genocide that will teach local young people, but will also be a resource for people outside Rwanda too. In addition, the centre will play a role in supporting survivors, many of whom are still traumatised following their experiences. There is also a very real need for some form of reconciliation to take place. Unlike other genocides that have taken place, in Rwanda, the perpetrators, or at least their families, still live in the same towns and villages as they always did, and remain therefore the neighbours of surviving victims or their relatives. To find a way to live together after such events is a painful and difficult process, but there is no choice. The Aegis Centre will attempt to play its small role in shaping the future within the locale in which it is placed.

Seminal works have already been written on the Rwandan genocide and its circumstances, yet a whole book remains to be written on the difficult post-genocide issues we currently face in Rwanda – and probably will be one day. In the meantime, it seems important that those who confront the Holocaust and care about its consequences listen to these drowned-out voices and see how we can help them. It is hoped that if the Aegis Centre in Rwanda is successful, it could be the first of a series of Aegis Centres around the world reflecting the ethos of Beth Shalom in the respective countries and bringing people together on these crucial challenges. Jack Cigman, founder of the Lapid Trust, identified that the work of Beth Shalom has an unusual message that could and should be adapted for different circumstances, to replace hatred and serve as an important educational and social service in places where genocide has occurred. The Lapid Trust is to partner Beth Shalom and Aegis in the development of the first centre to create a memorial that can be adapted or replicated many times over.

Building bridges between the real impact of genocide on real people's lives and our own cosseted existence is a task that takes concerted effort. Everyone needs to participate in this, right across the spectrum of our society. In the United Kingdom there are now many opportunities to bring people together to discuss and learn about the Holocaust and events that raise similar issues. Beth Shalom is part of a growing landscape of sites, museums and educational programmes dedicated to teaching about the Holocaust and ensuring that its memory and challenge stay in the public memory. The Imperial War Museum's Holocaust exhibition, the Anne Frank Trust, The Shoah Centre, the Spiro Institute, the Holocaust Educational Trust, the Jewish Museum and the Council of Christians and Jews all have active programmes of education which in different ways run alongside and relate to the work of Beth Shalom. Such relationships should, I believe, always be reciprocal and supportive of one another; not to be so would be to insult those we seek to commemorate. In turn, organisations around the world need to join forces to complement each other and benefit from the growth in research and education, creating shared goals. As the Beth Shalom Centre prepares to open to the public, we hope to be able to offer a meaningful and challenging experience to a broad spectrum of people from the Midlands and north of the country. There is an appetite among the general population to learn about the Holocaust, to understand both its historical occurrence and to engage with the difficult issues arising from it.

So too the launch and success of Holocaust Memorial Day in the UK has been a valuable development in encouraging more schools, local authorities, churches and individuals to engage in commemorating and learning about the Holocaust. It has been an enriching experience to work with colleagues in government departments who have clearly taken the interests of Holocaust Memorial Day so seriously and personally. Neil Frater and David Jones, who have worked on behalf of consecutive Home Secretaries to establish Holocaust Memorial Day, have demonstrated that it is possible to be a civil servant and to really care about the outcomes and consequences of one's work. It has been a real pleasure to work with them – although admittedly it never crossed my mind when creating Beth Shalom that we would need to speak to a government official about the Holocaust. Today, much of my time is spent doing so, indicating the real change that has taken place within government in addressing the Holocaust as an issue for British society. And, as one country after another recognises the importance of establishing days of remembrance and education, the hope is that eventually an entire generation will grow up knowing that the Holocaust happened and that it matters to them too.

As well as Holocaust Memorial Day, the Foreign and Commonwealth Office's delegation to the International Task Force for Holocaust Education, Remembrance and Research continues to play an active role. Currently headed by James Kidner, one of the most effective and energetic civil servants you will ever hope to meet, a delegation of the British Government, along with a number of UK Holocaust Organisations, has been working closely with partners in Lithuania.

My own role as Chair of the Memorials Working Group provides a challenge. The Task Force is attempting to document and provide support for the many thousands of sites and memorials across the European continent. Nearly sixty years after the end of the Second World War, there are still many Holocaust sites that are either unknown, unmarked or not sufficiently documented. Along with its Education and Academic working groups, the Task Force is trying to provide inter-governmental support for government departments and a host of non-governmental organisations like Beth Shalom right across the continent and further afield. In view of the task that lies ahead, it is important that remembrance and education create an inclusive and shared environment in the landscape of Holocaust memory, in which Beth Shalom is one part of a very significant whole.

The biggest danger now, with all the work that is happening, is that the Holocaust becomes over-exposed within British society, leading to its gradual normalisation. The more exposed people are to its message, the more complacent they are likely to become. Unlike in former occupied countries, the Holocaust is not embedded on the landscape of the English countryside. There are not former camps or deportation sites in every county, or places that Grandma remembers on every street corner, thankfully. But this also means that this is not our history in the sense that the landscape is permanently scarred with its memory. There are many connections to the history of the Holocaust engendered through Britain's role at that time, but it does not have the same historical, social and cultural impact as it does on the European mainland. Therefore the way in which we choose to remember the Holocaust has to find its connections to our past, and to then make the social, cultural and ethical connections to its implications. Even though it will always be an impressive and overwhelming chapter in our history books, this is the only way it will have an enduring presence in our lives.

In some respects, because of this detachment from the direct historical linkage, there are good grounds for arguing that the Holocaust should always and only be remembered voluntarily and at a grass roots level in the UK, so that ordinary people own both the narrative and the implications. That way, the spectrum of people who would benefit from its content can do so at a level which is appropriate to their environment. Whilst the history is the same history for everyone, each person or group has a different set of contexts and issues that condition their understanding of the Holocaust. They therefore need to be assisted in addressing these issues in a manner which is intelligible from their perspective. This should not result in its misappropriation (although this is always a danger), but in finding an appropriate way in and way forward for the group concerned. I am very often mindful when spending time with groups at Beth Shalom, of just how distinct their differing interests are, and therefore how ineffectual the visit would be if those interests were not addressed directly. There is an argument to say that if visitors come with preconceived notions that are not addressed or even challenged within a structured framework, they may well go away with negative concepts reinforced rather than changed. This is a situation we need to avoid, not only at the Beth Shalom centre, but in our national context too. Representing the Holocaust is never enough. We need to discuss its implications and challenge our own responses to it.

Beth Shalom is just one organisation. It will continue to grow and have its independent life. As it does so, it becomes abundantly clear that the work in which the Centre is involved is global and it will need many alliances and strategic partnerships to makes its message effective. Actually, it can only do its work in collaboration with many, many other people and organisations. The key, it seems, is finding the people with whom to work – those who can share the mission.

So, what next? The challenge has only just begun.

IN CONCLUSION

In conclusion, we still live in a world in which we might despair, a world in which the fragile beauty of living is senselessly shattered over and over again. A world in which terms like freedom, innocence, love, care, hope, peace and goodness are in the vocabulary of all, but not in the experience of enough. A world driven by material greed, political power and disregard for all but those inside the immediate circle in which we live. As we protect ourselves in our safe environments, even now somebody nearby is hurting from the effects of prejudice, of abuse or blatant victimisation. And somehow we have to live in this world. Somehow we must make it work.

When we dare to look back, we see a past littered with massacres, with crying children and ruined civilisations. When we reflect upon our present, we see how quickly, indeed how easily, we identify enemies, real or imagined. Time and again, we create the conditions in which we justify driving our neighbours from their homes, raping their women and killing their sons. Sometimes, depending on the circumstances, we call it war; at other times, genocide or ethnic cleansing. You may call it what you like, but when people are killed in the name of ideology, territory, power, race or religion, we have wasted lives. We have murdered someone who was meant to live, to enjoy everything that is beautiful about human existence and to die in peace. But then, within our troubled imaginations and paranoid temperaments, we justify and excuse and cover the cracks of the past. And then when we look to the future, just over the horizon we know that sooner or later someone else will become the victim of another's deluded fantasies. Somewhere, right now, there are ordinary people, with ordinary lives who, unbeknown to them, will soon become the victims of the next round of racial hate and persecution.

It is a deeply disturbing reality. This failure to arrest our impulse to inhumanity over and over again leads me toward a troubling cynicism. It taunts me to believe that the human condition cannot change. The senseless repetition of degrading and murderous injustices lead me to believe that pain and suffering and hurting hearts are an almost inevitable and integral part of human existence. And sadly, perhaps it's true.

But then, once in a while, in the midst of this debacle we call civilisation, there is something that can give us hope and a means to move forward. Something which enables us to see our way more clearly. In that moment, part of our past is made clear and the way to the future made more plausible. Perhaps we are afforded a glimpse into the dark soul of humanity, but given in some form the means to confront it. Such moments should bring us together, bridge our divided past and create the means to a shared and meaningful future for people of all backgrounds, faiths and convictions. In establishing Beth Shalom, we wanted to provide a place where a moment of such hope might be created for those who come. Not to gloss the past, but to confront it and find our way through the confusion of despair.

It would be good to go on to say, "So that all was not in vain," but of course it was all in vain because nothing can be gained from a tragedy so absolute, so soul-destroying and so final. And yet, while the lives of the Jews were wasted, in their honour we strive to learn about what they went through, and in their memory, we strive to learn from it too. Learning from it means taking whatever the 'lessons' are and ensuring that we put them into practice, without prejudice and every time. We talk of the 'lessons' of the Holocaust as if it were self-evident that 'it' should not occur again. But that is not a lesson. That is our hope. The lessons, I believe, lie within what we are prepared to do.

Beth Shalom and those who share in its vision are involved in a search to salvage something. It does not mean that that which is lost will be found again, or that those who still weep will ever find the solace they desire and surely deserve. It does not mean that anything that is past can be re-lived for a better outcome, because clearly it cannot be. It means that in spite of the despair, in spite of the broken hearts, in spite of the destruction and devastation, in spite of it all, the will to create a meaningful, if not hopeful, future can be found. It should be a future in which common understanding, compassion and care are shared across the boundaries of culture and religion and ethnicity.

Of course, we must be realistic; no single person, place or group of people are enough to effect the change that we need. In our varied institutions, in our churches and synagogues, in our homes and hearts, we often repeat the words "Never Again!", the sincerity of which should never be called into question. But what we mean by these words, and what we are prepared to do to ensure they become more than a cliché, is something we must continue to ask ourselves. In creating Beth Shalom, one of our goals was naturally to contribute to ensuring that such things are not repeated. But the means lie not in the cliché itself, but in talking, discussing and learning; in the choices we make and in changing the way we behave toward one another.

And so the journey we began in Jerusalem continues. It is a journey which has confronted us with many challenging and troubling facts about human existence. It has tested our human endurance, our Christian identity, our sense of past, present and future; but most of all, it has made us think about who we are, what we want to be, and what kind of world we want to pass on to our children.

I described much earlier my sense of utter devastation on visiting the mass grave at Zbylitowska Gora and feeling that we inhabit a broken world. That, I believe, is the case; the despair will never leave us; it is the despair of those who can never be consoled. However, I have come to recognise that there is an opportunity to inculcate the Jewish concept of *tikkun* (mending) from the Middle Ages, when the intercession of the righteous sages was thought to bring about the possibility of the reinstitution of the Temple in Jerusalem. In this case, to mend the world is for people of all walks of life to face the destruction and then to create a world of peace; it is to listen to the pain and anguish and then to find someone to console; it is to see the abandonment of the Jews and then always to remain vigilant; it is to see the hatred and to create understanding; it is to see the loss, and to create a world in which everyone is valued for who they are.

In the memorial hall at Beth Shalom we chose to put the words, "He who saves a single life, saves the world entire," from Pirkei Avot in the Talmud. These words were chosen for several reasons. Firstly, so that when we are working with people from across the spectrum of British life, of all ages and backgrounds, as we study the history of the Holocaust, we can further ask, "What difference might it have made if more people had been prepared to speak out and to save even a single neighbour or friend? By extension, we could also ask, "What difference might the avoidance of indifference make in our world today?"

The other reason we chose to put that all-important text around our hall was more personal. It was so that every time I go into that hall, which is virtually every day of my life, I also ask myself the question, "Would you have been courageous enough to have done that... and, more importantly, are you?"

GLOSSARY OF TERMS

Kotel: Literally, "wall". The *Kotel* referred to is a piece of the western wall of the Temple in Jerusalem, which has remained standing ever since the temple's destruction in 70 CE.

Erev Shabbat: Eve of Shabbat; ie, the period before sunset on Friday night which marks the start of *Shabbat* (the Sabbath).

Yarmulke: Head covering for observant Jewish males, also known as the *'kippa'* or skullcap. This head covering is worn as a sign of humility and an acknowledgement of God.

Mehitza: A physical barrier that keeps men and women apart in the synagogue, as an aid to the congregation's complete focus on worship.

Kvetl'ch: hand-written prayers to God, often left on the graves of respected individuals, in particular those of learned rabbis and teachers.

Bar Mitzvah: a ceremonial occasion marking the recognition of a young person as an adult in the Jewish community. Boys have *Bar Mitzvah* at 13 years of age and girls have *Bat Mitzvah* (also known as *Bat Chayl*) at 12 years of age.

Sheliach: representative of the State of Israel overseas, who works at a grassroots level to encourage Jewish communities to support and participate in the life of Israel.

Shul: synagogue, place of worship.

Matzevot: the plural of *Matzevah*, a Jewish tombstone.

Yeshivot: literally, 'Talmudic academies'; ie, Jewish colleges or schools, where students study Jewish law and tradition.

Mikvot: plural of *Mikvah*, the ritual bath. Bathing before and after particular events is an important Jewish religious custom.

Kosher: food prepared according to the requirements of Mosaic law.

Mezuzot: plural of *Mezuzah*, the small parchment containing the '*Shema*' prayer (Deuteronomy 6: 4-9) which is fixed in a small casing on the right doorpost of every entrance in a Jewish house.

Sukkot: the Feast of Tabernacles. A week-long celebration in the autumn, during which Jewish communities create and live in temporary booths or shelters to commemorate the forty years their ancestors spent wandering in the desert before reaching the Promised Land.

Ohel: a place where a person of note is buried with special honour. Similar in concept to a mausoleum, an *ohel* may be anything from a fenced-off area of the cemetery, to a special building over the *matzevah*.

Tzadikim: plural of *tzadik*; a righteous or esteemed pious man in the community. The term is generally only applied to rabbis of particular note, known for their wealth of wisdom or good deeds.

Yizkor: literally, 'remember'. The *Yizkor* prayer in memory of the dead is said four times a year.

Rebbe: the Yiddish term for 'Rabbi'.